THE PRINCIPAL TEACHINGS OF BUDDHISM

TSONGKAPA (1357–1419), also known as Je Rinpoche Lobsang Drakpa, is the single greatest commentator in the 2,500 year history of Buddhism. He was born in the district of Tsongka in eastern Tibet and took his first vows at a tender age. As a teenager he had already mastered much of the teachings of Buddhism and was sent by his tutors to the great monastic universities of central Tibet. Here he studied under the leading Buddhist scholars of his day; it is said as well that he enjoyed mystic visions in which he met and learned from different forms of the Buddha himself.

The 18 volumes of Tsongkapa's collected works contain eloquent and incisive commentaries on virtually every major classic of ancient Buddhism, as well as his famed treatises on the "Steps of the Path to Buddhahood." His students, who included the first Dalai Lama of Tibet, contributed hundreds of their own expositions of Buddhist philosophy and practice.

Tsongkapa founded the Great Three monasteries of Tibet, where by custom nearly 25,000 monks have studied the scriptures of Buddhism over the centuries. He also instituted the great Monlam festival, a period of religious study and celebration for the entire Tibetan nation. Tsongkapa passed away in his 62nd year, at his home monastery of Ganden in Lhasa, the capital of Tibet.

PABONGKA RINPOCHE (1878–1941), also known as Jampa Tenzin Trinley Gyatso, was born into a leading family in the state of Tsang in north-central Tibet. As a boy he entered the Gyalrong House of Sera Mey, one of the colleges of the great Sera Monastic University, and attained the rank of *geshe*, or master of Buddhist philosophy. His powerful public teachings soon made him the leading spiritual figure of his day, and his collected works on every facet of Buddhist thought and practice comprise some 15 volumes. His most famous student was

Kyabje Trijang Rinpoche (1901–1981), the junior tutor of the present Dalai Lama. Pabongka Rinpoche passed away at the age of 63 in the Hloka district of south Tibet.

GESHE LOBSANG THARCHIN (1921–) was born in Lhasa, and as a boy also entered the Gyalrong House of Sera Mey. He studied under both Pabongka Rinpoche and Kyabje Trijang Rinpoche, and after a rigorous 25-year course in the Buddhist classics was awarded the highest rank of the *geshe* degree. He graduated from the Gyumey Tantric College of Lhasa in 1958 with the position of administrator. Since 1959 he has taught Buddhist philosophy at various institutions in Asia and the United States, and in 1975 completed studies in English at Georgetown University. For 15 years he has served as the abbot of Rashi Gempil Ling, a Kalmuk Mongolian temple in New Jersey. He is the founder of the Mahayana Sutra and Tantra Centers of New Jersey and Washington D.C., and author of numerous translations of major Buddhist texts. In 1977 he directed the development of the first computerized Tibetan word processor, and has played a leading role in the re-establishment of Sera Mey Monastic College, of which he is a lifetime director.

MICHAEL PHILLIP ROACH (1952–) graduated with honors from Princeton University and received the Presidential Scholar medallion from Richard Nixon at the White House in 1970. He studied at the library of the Government of Tibet under the auspices of the Woodrow Wilson School of International Affairs, and then for over ten years under Geshe Tharchin at Rashi Gempil Ling, with additional course work at Sera Mey Monastic College. He is employed in the New York diamond industry and has been active in the restoration of Sera Mey, where he was ordained a Buddhist monk in 1983.

TSONGKAPA

The Principal Teachings of Buddhism

with a commentary by

PABONGKA RINPOCHE

translated by

GESHE LOBSANG THARCHIN

with

MICHAEL ROACH

PALJOR PUBLICATIONS

Published by :
PALJOR PUBLICATIONS
D- 39, Jangpura
New Delhi - 110014
An Imprint of
CLASSICS INDIA PUBLICATIONS
DELHI

Association with
The Mahayana Sutra and Tantra Press
216 A West Second Street
Freewood Acres
Howell, New Jersey 07731, USA
telephone (908) 367—5898

First Indian Edition 1998

Library of Congress Cataloging in Publication Data

Tson-kha-pa-Blo-bzan-grags-pa, 1357-1419
The Principal Teaching of Buddhism.
(Classics of Middle Asia)
Translation of: Lam gyi gtso bo rnam gsum.
Bibliography: p.
1. Tson-kha-pa Blo-bzan-grags-pa, 1357-1419.
Lam gyi gtso bo rnam gsum. 2. Buddhism—Doctrines.
3. Dge-lugs-pa (Sect)—Doctrines. 1. Pha-bon-
kha-pa Byams-pa-bstan-'dzin-'phrin-las-rgya-mtsho,
1878-1941. Rdo rje 'chan Pha bon kha pa
dpal bzan pos lam . . . English. 1989.
II. Tharchin, Sermey Geshe Lobsang, 1921-
III. Roach, Michael 1952—. IV. Title.
V. Series.
BQ7950. T754L34913 1989 249.3'923 88-063957
ISBN : 81-85132-18-6
Copyright © 1988 Geshe Lobsang Tharchin
and Michael Roach
All rights Reserved

CONTENTS

FOREWORD 1

THE PRELIMINARIES 29

   I.   The Lama and the Word 31
  II.   Why Learn the Three Principal Paths? 31
 III.   An Offering of Praise 38
 IV.   How to Take a Lama 40
  V.   A Pledge to Compose the Work 46
 VI.   Encouragement to Study 54

THE FIRST PATH: RENUNCIATION 57

  VII.   Why You Need Renunciation 59
 VIII.   Stopping Desire for This Life 61
  IX.   Stopping Desire for Future Lives 77
   X.   How to Know When You've
       Found Renunciation 88

THE SECOND PATH: THE WISH TO ACHIEVE
ENLIGHTENMENT FOR EVERY LIVING BEING 91

  XI.   Why You Need the Wish
       for Enlightenment 93
  XII.   How to Develop the Wish
       for Enlightenment 95
 XIII.   How to Know When You've Found
       the Wish for Enlightenment 107

THE THIRD PATH: CORRECT VIEW   109

    XIV.   Why You Need Correct View   111
    XV.   What is Correct View?   118
    XVI.   How to Know When Your Analysis
        is Still Incomplete   127
    XVII.   How to Know When Your Analysis
        is Complete   128
    XVIII.   A Unique Teaching of the
        "Implication" School   130

PRACTICE   135

    XIX.   Put Into Practice What You
        Have Learned   137

IN CONCLUSION   141

    XX.   The Conclusion of the Explanation   143

PRAYER   149
    XXI.   A Disciple's Prayer   151

A SECRET KEY   155

    XXII.   A Secret Key to the Three
        Principal Paths   157

NOTES   161
BIBLIOGRAPHY   197

FOREWORD

YESHE LOBSANG WAS sitting as usual, staring at the ceiling, with his mouth wide open. We were young monks in Sera, one of the greatest Buddhist monasteries of Tibet. We sat in long rows facing each other, chanting one of the holiest prayers of our religion—the *Offering to Lamas*.

He was a full ten feet away, still day-dreaming with the wide-open mouth. I was the class cut-up, smart, but with a mischievous streak that got worse around some of my irreverent playmates. Two were sitting with me, one to each side, and not concentrating much on the prayer either. I made them a bet that I could hit Yeshe Lobsang right in the mouth.

We had this game called *pakda*, which means "the arrow of dough." You take a little ball of barley dough and flick it with your middle finger. This was the sort of thing I was good at, since I didn't waste much time studying, as I was supposed to.

Yeshe Lobsang was still slack-jaw, giving a good target. As the chanting rose to a crescendo I took aim and fired—the dough ball not only reached his mouth but shot right through to the back, and made a tremendous satisfying THWOCK! sound as it hit. And so he starts choking and spitting, and my friends on each side are roaring with laughter.

Up comes the Gergen, our housemaster who's supposed to keep an eye on us young ones during the ceremonies, and spots the offenders (they're still laughing; I kept a good straight face through the whole thing). He carries a small stick for just such occasions, and begins laying it on them from the back of the row. They start crying but they can't stop laughing, and get a good beating, and Yeshe Lobsang is still choking, and I'm sitting like a good young monk and get away scot-free. They told me later it was worth the beating to see Yeshe Lobsang's face all screwed up, and they didn't bear me a grudge that I got off free.

This little scene was very typical of my early years at Sera. Like many Tibetan boys, I was put into the monastery at a young age—this was in 1928, when I was only seven. At first we miss our parents and brothers and sisters, but then again our house in the monastery was a wonderful place for a boy—we would be with about fifty other boys our own age, which made for tremendous entertainment when we could get away with it, and also a deep feeling of brotherhood as we passed through the rigorous 25-year course together, and finally graduated with the coveted degree of "geshe"—master of Buddhist learning.

My own house was Gyalrong, which was one of the larger of about fifteen houses in Sera Mey College, itself one of the three great divisions of Sera Monastery. At its peak, Sera had over 8,000 teachers and disciples studying the ancient books of Buddhist wisdom.

Our monastery was located just outside of Lhasa, the capital of Tibet, which is the mountainous kingdom surrounded by Mount Everest and the rest of the Himalayas, north of India and west of China. Although the Buddha was born in India, Tibet is where his complete teachings have survived up to the present day. They were brought to our country over a thousand years ago, translated carefully into our language and kept safe in our mountain monasteries, while in the outside world the Buddhist books and monasteries and monks themselves have nearly disappeared, advocates of total non-violence in a violent world.

We young monks were not so noble. My house tutor would send us up to the rock cliffs behind the monastery with buckets to fetch water from the spring there, and we would dawdle for hours. Sometimes we would tuck our feet into our maroon-colored robes and slide down the long boulders until the cloth was ripped to shreds, and again the housemaster would give us our lumps. Rock-throwing was a good way to waste time, and I remember once hitting a lizard, and killing him by accident, and feeling terrible regret. For we believe that all living creatures have feelings; that they seek to feel good and avoid pain the same way you and I do.

On our way back to the monastery, a favorite trick was to lay out tacks on the path leading into the front gate. Our country lay in sort of a pocket behind the Himalayas, and was not as cold as most people imagine the "Land of Snows" should be. Some of the monks enjoyed going barefoot, and we would stoop behind the wall near the gate, waiting for a victim. Our giggles would start breaking out even before his feet reached the tacks, and then we would race away, robes flapping and flying in the wind, before he could come and catch us.

Even at home I was not the model student. My house tutor, the one who usually teaches us reading and writing before we begin our formal philosophical studies, was Geshe Tupten Namdrol. He was very strict with me and the other boy who shared our rooms. This boy was a notorious goof-off, and started to affect me too. As we entered our first courses in Buddhist logic and debate, I went through all the motions—I gave my exams well, memorized what I was supposed to, and quickly grasped the principles of reasoning—but my heart wasn't in it. By the time we began the next course, twelve long years on the meaning of Wisdom, I had gained a rather bad reputation.

Around this time my house tutor was offered the abbotship of a monastery named Ganden Shedrup Ling, in the district of Hloka, fairly far south of the capital. It was a great honor, for the position had been granted by the Kashak—the High Council of the Tibetan Government—and approved personally by the Dalai

Lama, who is the great spiritual and temporal leader of our land. The post would bring with it a substantial income which I, as Geshe Namdrol's right-hand man, would share. Everyone thought this would be a good chance for me to get ahead and also bow out gracefully from the tough course of study that lay before me, and which it seemed I might never complete.

It was at this time that the glorious Pabongka Rinpoche, the author of the commentary you are about to read, came into my life. Like me he had as a young man taken his course of studies at the Sera Mey College of Sera Monastery; in fact, he was from the same house, Gyalrong.

Pabongka Rinpoche was born in 1878, at a town called Tsawa Li in the Yeru Shang district of the state of Tsang, north of Lhasa. His family were of the nobility and owned a modest estate called Chappel Gershi. As a child he exhibited unusual qualities and in his seventh year was taken before Sharpa Chuje Lobsang Dargye, one of the leading religious figures of the day.

The lama felt sure that the boy must be a reincarnated saint, and even went so far as to examine him to see if he were the rebirth of his own late teacher. He was not, but the sage foretold that if the child were placed in the Gyalrong House of Sera Mey College, something wonderful would happen with him in the future.

Later on, the youngster was found to be a reincarnation of the Changkya line, which included the illustrious scholar Changkya Rolpay Dorje (1717–1786).[1] The lamas of this line had done much teaching in the regions of Mongolia and China— even in the court of the Chinese emperor himself—and the name "Changkya" had very strong Chinese connotations. Already in those days the Tibetan government and people were sensitive to the pressures put on us by our powerful neighbor to the east, so the name "Changkya" was ruled out, and the boy declared to be "Pabongka" instead.

Pabongka, also known as Parongka, is a large and famous rock-formation about three miles' walk from our Sera Monastery. The very word "pabong" means in our language a large boulder, or mass of rock. The place is historically very important for Tibetans, for perched on top of the rock is the palace of Songtsen Gampo, the 7th-Century king who made Tibet one of the leading nations of Asia at the time, and who helped bring the first Buddhist teachings from India.

Until Songtsen Gampo's time, the Tibetans had no written language. The king, who desired that the great texts of Buddhism be translated into our language, sent a number of delegations to India with the charge of bringing back a written alphabet. Many of the young men who went died in the terrible rainy heat of the Indian plains and jungles, so different from our high Tibetan plateau, but the minister Tonmi Sambhota finally returned. He proceeded to create an alphabet and grammatical system that last to this day. And it is said that he performed this great labor in the palace of Songtsen Gampo, atop the cliffs of Pabongka.

Pabongka Rinpoche was actually the second Pabongka, for it was finally agreed to announce that he had been recognized as the reincarnation of the Kenpo (or abbot) of the small monastery atop the rock. For this reason he was sometimes referred to as "Pabongka Kentrul," or the "reincarnation of the abbot of Pabongka." Pabongka Rinpoche's full name, by the way, was Kyabje Pabongkapa Jetsun Jampa Tenzin Trinley Gyatso Pel Sangpo, which translates as the "lord protector, the one from Pabongka, the venerable and glorious master whose name is the Loving One, Keeper of the Buddha's Teachings, Ocean of the Mighty Deeds of the Buddha." He is also popularly known as "Dechen Nyingpo," which means "Essence of Great Bliss" and refers to his mastery of the secret teachings of Buddhism. We Tibetans feel that it is disrespectful to refer to a great religious leader with what we call his "bare" name—such as "Tsongkapa" or "Pabongka"— but we have tried here to simplify the Tibetan names to help our Western readers.

Pabongka Rinpoche's career at Sera Mey College was not outstanding; he did finish his geshe degree, but reached only the "lingse" rank, which means that he was examined just at his own monastery and did not go on for one of the higher ranks such as "hlarampa." The *hlarampa* level requires an exhausting series of public examinations and debates at different monasteries, culminating in a session before the Dalai Lama and his teachers at the Norbulingka summer palace. It was only after his graduation from Sera Mey, and the success of his teaching tours through the countryside outside the capital, that Pabongka Rinpoche's fame started to spread. Gradually he began to build up a huge following and displayed tremendous abilities as a public teacher. He was not tall (as I remember about my height, and I am only 5'6"), but he was broad-chested and seemed to fill the entire teaching throne when he climbed up on it to begin his discourse.

His voice was incredibly powerful. On frequent occasions he would address gatherings of many thousands of people, yet everyone could hear him clearly (in those days in Tibet we had never heard of microphones or loudspeakers). Part of the trick of course was to pack the audience in Tibetan-style, cross-legged on the floor, with the lama on an elevated platform. Still the audience would flow out onto the porch of the hall, and sit perched above on the roof, watching through the steeple windows.

Pabongka Rinpoche had an uncanny ability to relate to his audience, and for this reason he became a teacher for the common man as well as for us monks. Generally speaking, the majority of the Buddha's teachings as we learn them in the monastery are extremely detailed, deep and sometimes technical. Moreover, we use rigorous tests of formal logic to analyze them as we move up through our classes. These methods are important for gaining the highest goals of Buddhist practice in a systematic way, and for passing these teachings on to others. But they were beyond the abilities and time of many of our Tibetan laymen. The Rinpoche's great accomplishment was that he found a way to attract and lead listeners of every level.

His most famous weapon was his humor. Public discourses in Tibet could sometimes go on for ten hours or more without a break, and only a great saint could keep his attention up so long. Inevitably part of the audience would start to nod, or fall into some reverie. Then Pabongka Rinpoche would suddenly relate an amusing story or joke with a useful moral, and send his listeners into peals of laughter. This would startle the daydreamers, who were always looking around and asking their neighbors to repeat the joke to them.

The effects on his audience were striking and immediate. I remember particularly the case of Dapon Tsago, a member of the nobility who held a powerful position equivalent to Minister of Defense. Public teachings in Tibet were as much social as religious affairs, and aristocrats would show up in their best finery, often it seemed not to hear the dharma but rather to put in an appearance. So one day this great general marches in to the hall, decked out in silk, his long hair flowing in carefully tailored locks (this was considered manly and high fashion in old Tibet). A great ceremonial sword hung from his belt, clanging importantly as he swaggered in.

By the end of the first section of the teaching he was seen leaving the hall quietly, deep in thought—he had wrapped his weapon of war in a cloth to hide it, and was taking it home. Later on we could see he had actually trimmed off his warrior's locks, and finally one day he threw himself before the Rinpoche and asked to be granted the special lifetime religious vows for laymen.

Thereafter he always followed Pabongka Rinpoche around, to every public teaching he gave.

The Rinpoche had never spent much time at the small monastery atop the Pabongka rock, and his fame soon reached such proportions that the Ngakpa College of Sera Monastery offered him a large retreat complex on the hillside above Pabongka. The name of this hermitage was Tashi Chuling, or "Auspicious Spiritual Isle." There were some sixty Buddhist monks in residence there, and as I remember about sixteen personal attendants who helped the Lama with his pressing schedule: two monk-secretaries, a manager for finances, and so on. The Rinpoche would divide his time between his quarters here and a small meditation cell built around the mouth of a cave, further up the side of the mountain.

The cave was known as Takden, and it was here that Pabongka Rinpoche would escape for long periods to do his private practice and meditations. The central chamber had a high vaulted ceiling, so high that the light of a regular fire-torch could not even reach it, and the darkness seemed to go up forever. In the center of the ceiling there was an odd natural triangle in the rock, which looked exactly like the outer shape of one of the mystic worlds described in our secret teachings.

In the corner of this wonderful cave, an underground spring flowed from a rock — and above it was another natural drawing, this one just like the third eye that we see painted on the forehead of one of our female Buddhas. By the way, this "third eye" you hear about is largely metaphorical, and stands for the spiritual understanding in one's heart. We believed the cave was home for a *dakini* — sort of a Buddhist angel — because people often said they saw a wondrous lady come from the cave, but no one had ever seen her enter.

It was in his private quarters at the Tashi Chuling hermitage that I first met Pabongka Rinpoche. He had been away on an extended teaching tour in eastern Tibet, and just returned. I was still the wild teenager and had been stuck with the distasteful job of *nyerpa* for Gyalrong House — this means I was a kind of quartermaster and had to make sure there was enough firewood and food to keep the house kitchen going for several hundred monks. Since the Rinpoche was a member of Gyalrong, we were supposed to send a committee over to the hermitage to welcome him back and present him gifts. As *nyerpa* I was expected to arrange some supplies and help carry them along.

In private conversation Pabongka Rinpoche was in the habit of constantly attaching "Quite right! Quite right!" to everything he said. So I distinctly remember when I came into his presence, and he put his hand on my head, and he said "Quite right! Quite right! Now this one looks like a bright boy!" From that day on I felt as though I had received his blessing, and some special power to pursue my studies.

In my eighteenth year, the Rinpoche was requested to come across to our own Sera Mey College and deliver a discourse on the Steps of the path to Buddhahood. He would receive countless requests of this sort, usually from wealthy patrons who hoped to collect some merit for the future life, or from monks who wanted to receive the transmission of a particular teaching so they could pass it on to their own followers in the future. The Rinpoche would usually promise to consider the request, and then try to satisfy several at one time by delivering a large public discourse.

These discourses would be announced months in a advance. The sponsors would rent a huge assembly hall in one of the major monasteries just outside the capital, or reserve one of the great chapels in Lhasa itself. We monks had our regular classes to attend but could sometimes arrange to make the hour's walk to Lhasa (no cars in Tibet those days), attend the teaching, and walk back quickly before the evening debate sessions at the monas-

tery park. I remember the elderly monks would start out
before us and return later, or even get permission to take
a room in Lhasa for the duration of the course, since the
walk was difficult for them.

This particular discourse at Sera Mey went on for a full
three months. We sat for six hours a day: three hours in
the morning, with a break for lunch, and then three
hours in the afternoon. Pabongka Rinpoche went carefully through the entire *Lam Rim Chenmo,* the great
exposition of the entire Steps on the path to Buddhahood written by the incomparable Lord Tsongkapa — who
is also the author of the root verses explained by
Pabongka Rinpoche in his commentary here. The Rinpoche referred to all eight of the classic texts on the Steps
of the path during his discourse, which was attended by
about 10,000 monks.

Like so many others in the audience, I was stunned by
the power of his teaching. Most of it I had heard before,
but the way in which he taught it and, I felt, the blessing
I had received from him made it suddenly strike home
for me. Here I was, living the short precious life of a
human, and fortunate enough to be a student at one of
the greatest Buddhist monasteries in the world. Why was
I wasting my time? What would happen if I suddenly
died?

In my heart I made a decision to master the teachings,
for the benefit of myself and others. I remember going to
my room, to my house teacher Geshe Namdrol, and
declaring my change of heart to him: "Now the bad boy
is going to study, and become a master geshe!" Geshe
Namdrol laughed, and told me, "The day you become a
geshe is the day I become the Ganden Tripa!"

Now the Ganden Tripa is one of the highest religious
personages in Tibet: he holds the throne of Lord
Tsongkapa himself, and wins the position by attaining
the highest rank of geshe — the *hlarampa* — and then serv-
ing as the head of one of the two colleges devoted to the

study of the secret teachings. My house teacher had never gone above the *tsokrampa* rank of geshe, so could never have become the Ganden Tripa anyway, and we both knew it. I got angry, in a good way, and swore to him that I would not only become a geshe but a *hlarampa* geshe as well. In my later years, after I had passed the *hlarampa* examinations with highest honors, Geshe Namdrol used to come a little sheepishly and ask in a roundabout way if I could help him pick a good topic for the day's debates.

This was the great gift I received from Pabongka Rinpoche: I attacked my studies with a passion, keeping my mind on the shortness of life and the value of helping others. Up to this time I had been the house scribe, sort of a clerk who wrote everyone's letters home. To save time for my studies I took my costly pens and paper one day and, in front of my hundreds of house-mates, gave them away to anyone who would take them.

Then things got serious with the government's plan to send Geshe Namdrol and me to the monastic post in south Tibet. The tenure of the position would be six years, and I calculated my potential loss: one remaining year in the "special topics" class for the perfection of wisdom, two years in the class on the "middle way" or correct view, and the final two years in the classes on transcendent knowledge and vowed morality—all extremely important Buddhist topics. It took some courage, but I went to my teacher and begged his permission to stay and continue my studies at Sera Mey.

To everyone's amazement he agreed, and chose my happy-go-lucky roommate to accompany him instead. He turned over to me the keys to his apartments and left, much to the dismay of all our neighbors, who were convinced I would destroy the entire place. Soon though they were calling me "Gyalrong Chunze"—something like the "bookworm from Gyalrong House"—and my studies had improved enough that I was able to obtain a *miksel,* or special release from all other duties so I could devote every minute to my course work.

I can say it was here that my life turned around, for three reasons: Pabongka Rinpoche had put some renunciation and other good motivation in my heart; I had given up wealth and position to pursue spiritual studies; and I had gained the free time to devote myself to practice. In this last category of leisure I would include the fact that I finally got out from under the influence of my prankster roommate, and also had the good fortune to meet the Venerable Jampel Senge.

As monastic custom goes, Jampel Senge's class (which was a year ahead of mine) had been joined with my own at a certain point in the curriculum. Like some of the famous figures mentioned in the teaching you are about to read, he was originally brought up in a different religion and came to our monastery rather late in his life, a confirmed skeptic. He stayed though and became a real master of Buddhism; every day we would spend hours together, reviewing what we had heard in class and preparing each other for the evening debates. It was from Jampel Senge that I learned the value of good spiritual friends; in the end, we reached the highest ranks of the geshe together. After our country was lost he travelled to Italy, where he became the tutor of the famed Tibetologist professor Tucci, and finally passed away there.

It was well before my final exams that the precious Pabongka Rinpoche himself passed from this earth. After the teachings I attended at Sera Mey, the Rinpoche had travelled to the Hloka district in south Tibet, to instruct his many disciples there. He continued on to the province of Dakpo, teaching continuously, and passed away there at the age of sixty-three, in 1941. It is a custom in our country to cremate the body of a holy person and preserve the ashes in a small shrine, and I still remember the day when they brought the Rinpoche's remains back to his mountain hermitage, Tashi Chuling. A shrine was constructed and a great many monks including myself came to pay our respects, and make our final offerings.

We Buddhists believe that although the body dies, the mind — since it is not destructible like physical matter — continues on and eventually comes into a new body, within your mother's womb if you are to be born as a human. We believe that great saints can select their birth, and that out of compassion they will choose to return and teach their disciples again if this will benefit them. Thus it is a custom for the disciples to seek the help of some great wise men and go out to find the child who is the reincarnation of their teacher.

Pabongka Rinpoche's first reincarnation was born in the Drikung area of central Tibet, during the troubled years when the Chinese first invaded and began to take over our country. He escaped along with many of our people over the Himalaya mountains, and came down into the Indian plain. Here most of the monks who survived the perilous journey were placed by the Indian government in a makeshift refugee camp set up in the abandoned prison at Buxall, in the jungles of Bengal state, west India. (I myself was nearly killed during the bombardment of our monastery, and upon reaching India was chosen by His Holiness the Dalai Lama to work in the newly-formed education office of the exile government at Dharamsala, near the border of north India.)

Buxall Prison had been built many years before by the British during their rule of India. It was a massive structure of concrete and huge iron doors built purposely in the middle of nowhere. Mahatma Gandhi and Mr. Nehru, the leaders of India's movement for independence, had been among the distinguished inmates.

India is a poor country but did her best to help us refugees; the prison was the only immediate housing they could find in their overpopulated land. The jungle weather was hot, steamy and humid — the complete opposite of our homeland. Like the delegations of translators who had come to India over a thousand years before to bring us back an alphabet, the majority of our monks came down with tuberculosis and other tropical diseases. A great many died.

Buxall Prison did have one advantage though—total solitude. And for the first time in history, great scholars from all the many traditions and monasteries of Tibet were thrown together in one place, for over a decade. In this environment the second Pabongka Rinpoche excelled in his studies, and before long was himself teaching the other monks such subjects as grammar and composition. He stood for his geshe examination at an early age, and distinguished himself. During these examinations he seemed weak and in some pain, and immediately after their completion was hospitalized with a serious case of tuberculosis. To the dismay of all the monks he suddenly died; his close followers could not believe that he would choose to leave them at such a desperate hour in our history—we were thrown into depression, and one great geshe even tried to kill himself (although we do believe that this is a sin).

The second reincarnation of Pabongka Rinpoche was discovered in Darjeeling, India, by his disciple Kyabje Trijang Rinpoche and is now a promising young monk at the new Sera Monastery, which was founded in south India by a dedicated band of refugee monks who survived the ordeal at Buxall. He lives in comfortable quarters that were constructed by his followers, some of whom also attended him in his two previous lives. His principal tutor was the late Giku-la, Lobsang Samten, who also served as a leader of the new Gyalrong House and director of the Sera Mey Scholarship Fund, which I and my own students have established for the continued training of young monks in our traditional course of study.

The original Pabongka Rinpoche also survives in the labors of his principal disciples, and in his numerous writings. His collected works comprise some fifteen volumes with a total of about a hundred different treatises covering a wide range of topics from both the open and the secret teachings of the Buddha. His students played a special role in preserving his teachings, as many of the major works that we have today are actually records of his oral discourses compiled by his closest followers. The commentary on the Three Principal Paths here, for example, was prepared from a collection of lecture notes by the Venerable Lobsang Dorje. The Rinpoche's great work on the Steps of the path to Buddhahood, entitled *Liberation in Our Hands,* was compiled by Kyabje Trijang Rinpoche, Lobsang Yeshe Tenzin Gyatso, who served as one of the two tutors of the present Dalai Lama and was my own precious root lama. Kyabje Trijang Rinpoche has left us with a detailed biography of Pabongka Rinpoche, in two volumes, along with some nine lengthy volumes of his own masterly composition. It is at Trijang Rinpoche's direction too that I have undertaken an English translation of *Liberation in Our Hands,* and the first volume will be published this year.

Over many centuries, Tibet has produced an extraordinary number of Buddhist saints and scholars; therefore it is rare for a lama's teachings to become classics within his own lifetime, as did the works of Pabongka Rinpoche. Certainly another exception to this rule was the matchless Je Tsongkapa, the author of the original verses of the *Three Principal Paths* in the present volume.

Lord Tsongkapa's full name is Gyalwa Je Tsongkapa Chenpo Lobsang Drakpa, and he holds a unique position in our Tibetan Buddhist tradition. All in one he was the greatest philosopher, and most eloquent writer, and most successful organizer of Buddhism who ever lived in our land; as time continues to pass after the forced opening of our country's doors, I feel sure he will come to be recognized throughout the world as one of the greatest thinkers in history.

He was born in 1357 in the Amdo area of northeast

Tibet, in a district called Tsongka (hence his name, which means "the one from Tsongka"). He was granted his first, basic vows at a tender age from one Chuje Karmapa Rolpay Dorje, and received the name Kunga Nyingpo. By the age of eight he had taken his vows as a Buddhist novice, and already received initiations into the secret teachings of Buddhism. He excelled in his studies and on the advice of his teachers journeyed to central Tibet in his sixteenth year, to seek further instruction from the many sages there.

It would be impossible to relate here all of what Je Tsongkapa then studied. Briefly put, he mastered the entire open and secret teachings of Buddhism, as well as the various classical sciences. A few examples of the subjects he covered with different teachers are: the secret teachings of Naro and the Great Seal from Chen-nga Chukyi Gyalpo; the ancient medical traditions from Je Konchok Kyab; the perfection of wisdom from masters at Dewa Chen Monastery, the great Sakya teacher Rendawa, and Nyawon Kunga Pel; the Steps of the path and other Seer precepts from Hle Rinpoche; classical logic from Lochen Dunsang, Venerable Rendawa, and Dorje Rinchen; the treasure of knowledge from Lochen Dunsang and Venerable Rendawa; the middle way from Venerable Rendawa and Kenchen Chukyab Sangpo; older sutras from Kenchen Losel; vowed morality from Venerable Rendawa and Master Chukyab Sangpo; the secret teachings of the wheel of time from Yeshe Gyeltsen and others; those on the secret collection from Venerable Rendawa, as well as from Hle Rinpoche and others, according to the system of their own teacher, Buton Rinpoche; the "blue book" of the Seer masters, the deeds of bodhisattvas, and early mental training texts from Kenchen Chukyab Sangpo; and the list goes on and on.

This does not include all the teachings that Lord Tsongkapa is said to have received directly from enlightened beings through dreams, visions, and direct contact;

we read for example that for many years he was tutored by the divine being Gentle Voice. At first one of his principal teachers, Lama Umapa, acted as sort of a translator; later on, Lord Tsongkapa was able to meet and learn from this being on his own.

We should say a word here about these "divine beings." We Buddhists believe that there are many Buddhas in the universe, and that they can each appear on one or more planets at the same time, if this will help the beings who live there. We believe that a Buddha is the ultimate evolution of all life; that he can know all things, but does not have all power: he did not create the universe, for example (this we have done by the force of our own past deeds, good and bad), nor can he take all our sufferings away from us by himself—these too we believe come from our own past actions, and must be stopped by ourselves.

We do believe that by studying and practicing the teaching of the Buddha we ourselves can become Buddhas, as can every living being. Therefore when we speak of enlightened beings appearing to a saint directly and so on we do not mean that Buddhists believe in a great many gods or the like, but rather that any being who has removed all his suffering and gained all knowledge can appear to any one of us, in any form that may help us to reach this ultimate state ourselves.

Only after he had received a great many teachings did Lord Tsongkapa take his full ordination as a monk; this was in Yarlung, south of Lhasa, when he was twenty-five. The ordination name he had already been granted, upon becoming a novice, was Lobsang Drakpa—and it is in Lord Tsongkapa's memory that so many Tibetans are given "Lobsang" as their personal name.

By now his transition from student to teacher was accelerating quickly, and in fact he later tutored a number of his own greatest teachers. We can understand his life from this point on more clearly if we look at the influence his teaching still has on Buddhism today, rather than simply retracing his career up to the final moment at Ganden Monastery in 1419, when he passed away at the age of sixty-two.

Buddhism is counted among the handful of great religions in the modern world, but it is actually close to extinction. In some countries it has disappeared, only recently, through violent political upheavals. In other countries it remains, but typically not in its whole form: the Buddha taught the so-called "greater" and "lesser" ways, contained in four great schools of thought, and all four of these are now studied and practiced actively only in the Tibetan tradition. This tradition itself survives mainly in our monastic universities; among these, the three great institutions of Ganden, Drepung, and Sera are the mainstays. We can learn much of the adult years of Lord Tsongkapa by searching for his influence upon these last great bastions of the total Buddhist path.

And in fact we see his hand here everywhere. A young monk at Sera Monastery, for example, begins his formal education with the study of logic, and as his textbook is likely to use either the *Path to Freedom* or the *Jewel of Reasoning*. Both were written by direct disciples of Lord Tsongkapa: the former by Gyaltsab Je (1362–1432), and the latter by Gyalwa Gendun Drup (1391–1475).

For his next course, twelve years on what we call the "perfection of wisdom," our monk will be using the *Golden Rosary*, a commentary composed by the Master at Kyishu and Dewa Chen, following his final ordination. The monk will refer as well to the immense *Essential Jewel*, another work by Gyaltsab Je. When he reaches the "special topics" part of the course, he may well commit to memory the entire 230 pages of Lord Tsongkapa's *Essence of Eloquence*, on certain tenets of the great Buddhist schools.

Between courses the young monk will often have opportunities to attend discourses delivered by visiting lamas; perhaps by the Dalai Lama himself. The present is the fourteenth of his line and, as we might expect, the first was another of Lord Tsongkapa's direct disciples. Popular subjects for these public discourses are the *Greater Steps on the Path* (by Lord Tsongkapa), *The Bodhisattva's Life* (Gyaltsab Je's *Door for Bodhisattvas* is likely to be the commentary used), or the *Three Principal Paths* (our present text, again by Lord Tsongkapa).

The monk student's next course will be the very difficult "middle way" philosophy of the highest school of Buddhism. He will be using Lord Tsongkapa's *Great Commentary* for understanding the early Indian commentaries. If he goes deeper, the monk might read *Eye-Opener,* the great exposition on emptiness by Kedrup Je (1385–1438), again a direct disciple of Lord Tsongkapa.

Everywhere the young scholar goes he is surrounded by the Master's influence. The very monastery in which he walks has been founded either by Lord Tsongkapa or one of his direct disciples: Ganden in 1409 by the Lord himself, Drepung in 1416 by Jamyang Chuje Tashi Pelden, and Sera in 1419 by Jamchen Chuje Shakya Yeshe. The very robes that the monk wears were in part designed by Lord Tsongkapa. When he sits down in his room to meditate, he is likely to start off with a mental picture of the Master, as taught in a popular *Lama Practice* manual. When he fingers his beads, he may well be counting *miktsema's,* the Tibetan equivalent of Hail Mary's, in supplication to Lord Tsongkapa.

And the monk will eventually take his geshe examinations at the great Monlam Festival, a national three-week holiday devoted to spiritual activities and instituted by Lord Tsongkapa in 1408. If he is Mongolian, he will probably count his birthday from the great Festival of Lights on the 25th of the tenth Asian month: a day devoted to the memory of Lord Tsongkapa.

If he gets that far, our monk's next course covers what we call the "treasure of knowledge." His basic commentary will be that of the first Dalai Lama, Lord Tsongka-pa's student. By now the monk is a master logician, and can use the *Gyalwang Treasure,* a dialectic exposition composed by Gyalwang Trinley Namgyal about a hundred years ago. This author is famous too for writing the *Great Biography*—of Lord Tsongkapa.

Throughout his course work, the student attends daily debate sessions; he goes to an open park at the monastery and must defend his understanding of the day's lesson, quoting the texts from memory since no books may be brought along. Here he is again following the example of the monk from Tsongka, who travelled to central Tibet as a teenager and distinguished himself in a great many public debates at the monasteries of Dewa Chen, Sakya, Sangden, Gakrong, Damring, Eh, Nenying, and others.

If he passes his geshe examination with honors, the monk will be eligible to attend one of the two tantric colleges, where he will learn the secret teachings of Buddhism. One of his principal textbooks will be the *Greater Steps on the Secret Path,* by Lord Tsongkapa himself. He may too use one of the many detailed treatises of Kedrup Je, another of the Master's illustrious students. The collected writings of Lord Tsongkapa and his two major disciples are usually printed together under the title "Collected Works of the Father and his Sons." They run no less than thirty-eight large volumes containing some 300 different treatises on every subject of Buddhist philosophy. Lord Tsongkapa's composition is marked by extensive references to the early classics of Buddhism, a strict use of the rules of logic and precise definitions, a massive vocabulary of Tibetan which will probably never be equalled, a flawless observance of the rules of classical grammar, and a sensitivity to the needs of students of every level—from beginning to advanced.

This last point is why the present work, the *Three Principal Paths,* has been so popular in Tibet over the centuries. As the commentary here describes, Lord

Tsongkapa has managed to pack the entire teachings of Buddhism into a mere fourteen verses. We believe that, if the work is studied with a pure heart and the right effort, it can actually lead one to enlightenment.

As its closing lines reveal, the text of the *Three Principal Paths* was written by Lord Tsongkapa for a student of his by the name of Ngawang Drakpa, whom we also know as Tsako Wonpo—the "friar from Tsako district." Ngawang Drakpa was not one of Lord Tsongkapa's most famous students, although a wonderful drawing of him does appear in the group of close disciples clustered around the Master in the central painting of the *Tsongka Gyechu*, a traditional rendering of the life of Lord Tsongkapa in a standard set of fifteen scroll-paintings.[2]

Surprisingly, one of the best sources we have for information about Ngawang Drakpa is the biography of Pabongka Rinpoche, the author of our commentary here. In the first volume of the work we come across a captivating exchange between the Rinpoche and his mother, who has shown up at Sera Monastery and is dismayed by the austerity of his life there. She wonders out loud how things might have been if the world had recognized the boy for what he was—the reincarnation of the great Changkya, who had served as personal spiritual advisor to the Emperor of China some 200 years before, and whose luxurious quarters still waited near the palace in Peking, for the next incarnation. But Pabongka Rinpoche says to her,

I don't see how I can say that I've ever shown even the slightest trace of the good qualities that Changkya Rolpay Dorje used to have: his knowledge and his spiritual attainments. I will admit though that I feel tremendous faith and admiration for this great man, and when I read his works, they are definitely easier for me to grasp than other scriptures. It is true too that ever since I was young I have had some strong attraction to the kind of Chinese sedan chair in which Changkya used to ride, and a tremendous predilection for all things Chinese.

This and the fact that you, mother, used to talk so much about how I was recognized as him have led me to wonder if I might not really be Changkya—and I begin sometimes to identify myself with him.

On occasion too the thought comes to my mind that I have been other people as well, in other times . . . during the days when our great and gentle protector Tsongkapa lived on this earth I was, I sometimes think, that friar from Tsako—Ngawang Drakpa.[3]

Because of this revelation, the author of Pabongka Rinpoche's biography relates something of the life of Ngawang Drakpa. We see one scene in the paintings of Lord Tsongkapa's life where he is teaching a group of four monks at a temple named Keru, and in the description of the great Jamyang Shepa (1648–1721) we read that the Master is imparting lessons on the topics of the perfection of wisdom, logic, and the middle way to Ngawang Drakpa and his classmates.[4] This seems to be just after Lord Tsongkapa's ordination, and well before the first contact with his three more famous disciples: Gyaltsab Je, Kedrup Je, and the first Dalai Lama.

Pabongka Rinpoche's biographer concurs and quotes a *Secret Biography* to the effect that Ngawang Drakpa belonged to a group of the Master's pupils named the "Original Four," previous to his period of seclusion. Ngawang Drakpa is here said to have been born into the line of the kings of Tsako, to the far east of Tibet in Gyalmo Rong. This is another name for Gyalrong, which is also the very house at Sera Mey College where the child Pabongka was placed, on the sage's advice.

We read that Ngawang Drakpa, like Lord Tsongkapa himself, travelled to central Tibet in search of further instruction. He became adept in both the open and secret teachings, met and learned from the Master, and accompanied him on a journey to the Tsel monastery in Kyishu, a district in east Tibet. After their return to Lhasa, the capital, he undertook various spiritual practices.

One well-known story about Ngawang Drakpa says that around this time he and his teacher agreed to take special notice of their dreams during the coming night. Ngawang Drakpa dreamt that he gazed to the sky and saw two great white conch-shells, the kind we hollow out in Tibet and use as horns in our religious ceremonies. The shells descended into the lap of his robes, and suddenly merged into one.

Ngawang Drakpa saw himself taking up the conchhorn and blowing it—the sound that came out was deafening, and spread to an inconceivable distance. Lord Tsongkapa interpreted the dream for his student, saying that it foretold how Ngawang Drakpa himself would spread the Buddha's teachings in his faraway home of Gyalrong. This in fact he did, for he is credited with founding over a hundred monasteries in eastern Tibet.

Pabongka Rinpoche's biography also speaks of the close relationship between this particular disciple and Lord Tsongkapa. In the final lines of the *Three Principal Paths,* the Master calls him "my son," showing a personal affection not very typical of the great scholar. He also seemed especially willing to satisfy Ngawang Drakpa's petitions for teachings (in the scene at Keru Temple we see some of the monks in a pleading gesture before the Master), and it is said that he composed his account of the famous bodhisattva Ever-Weeping at Ngawang Drakpa's personal request.[5]

As final evidence of their deep bond, our biographer quotes from a letter that Lord Tsongkapa sent his student. From the context (the entire message is still extant), we know that Ngawang Drakpa has already taken the long journey back to Gyalrong, and is making tremendous efforts to teach the people there. In these few beautiful lines,[6] the Master implores his disciple to follow his private instructions. He urges him to act and pray, in all his lives, as his teacher does. And he invites Ngawang Drakpa to meet him again, at the end, in enlightenment—where he promises to offer his favored student the first sip of their cup of immortality.

The ending of our own story is not as happy; we are refugees from Tibet, driven out of our Shangrila by the Chinese armies. The halls of Gyalrong house, where Pabongka Rinpoche gained his knowledge and I played my tricks on Yeshe Lobsang, have been bombed out and burned. The Rinpoche's mountain hermitage, Tashi Chuling, stands like some strange skeleton—only the front wall of stone remains erect, for all the rest was ripped down by the Chinese for firewood. The monk's cell at the mouth of his wonderful meditation cave, Takden, was smashed to rubble, which so fills the opening that no one can even find it now.

As Buddhists, we Tibetans do not feel anger at the Chinese, only a deep sadness at the loss of our country and traditions, and the deaths of over a million of our friends and relatives. In a way we have become more aware of how precious and short life is, and how we should practice religion while we are still alive to do so. Our loss too is perhaps the greater world's gain, as teachings like the one you are about to read now reach the outer world for the first time. I pray that this little book will help us all, to defeat our real enemies — the emotions of like and dislike and ignorance within our own minds.

Sermey Geshe Lobsang Tharchin	May 31, 1988
Baksha (Abbot)	15th day of the 4th
Rashi Gempil Ling	Buddhist month,
First Kalmuk Buddhist Temple	Sagan Dawa,
Freewood Acres, Howell	the day of the
New Jersey, USA	Buddha's Enlightenment

THE THREE PRINCIPAL PATHS

Herein kept is the "Key that Unlocks the Door to the Noble Path,"[7] a record that was made when teachings on the Three Principal Paths were imparted by the glorious Pabongka Rinpoche, the Holder of the Diamond.[8]

"Namo guru Manjugoshaya"—*I bow to the Master of Wisdom, whose name is Gentle Voice.*

I bow first to my teacher, who out of unmatched
kindness masquerades
In the saffron robe,[9] though in truth he's the
secret three of every Victor.[10]
Next I pledge I'll try to write here some
brief notes in explanation
Of the verses taught by Gentle Voice[11]
himself: "Three Principal Paths."[12]

THE PRELIMINARIES

I. THE LAMA AND THE WORD

NOW THERE WAS a lama, who was the very image of all the knowledge, love, and power of every single one of the absolute myriad of Buddhas. All in one person. Even for those who had never met him he was the single greatest friend that any of them, high or humble, could ever hope to have. He stood at the center of our universe, the holy Lama, one and only protector of all around him in these degenerate days. He was the great Holder of the Diamond, Pabongka Rinpoche, whose kindness knew no match. And from his holiest lips he spoke a teaching.

He spoke of the very heart of the "Steps to Buddhahood," a teaching which is itself the heart of all that is taught by each and every Buddha, of the past or present or future. He spoke of the Three Principal Paths, the nectar essence of all the wonderful words ever uttered by the Master, Gentle Voice.

Over the years, Pabongka Rinpoche imparted this profound instruction to us a number of times. He followed the original verses closely and savored the teaching well, wrapping within it every deep and vital point. Fearing we would forget some part we took down notes, and have gathered a number of them together from various sources, to make a single work.

II. WHY LEARN THE THREE PRINCIPAL PATHS?

Pabongka Rinpoche opened his teaching with introductory remarks that started off from a number of lines by the great Tsongkapa, King of the Dharma[13] in all three realms.[14] The first one read, "More than a wishing jewel, this life of opportunity."[15] By using these lines, the Rinpoche was able to tie his opening remarks to the

31

entire path from beginning to end, summarizing a number of important points in brief.

These began with the need for us in the audience to truly try to change our hearts, and listen to the teaching with the purest of motivations. We were to avoid with special care the three famous "problems of the pot,"[16] and to follow the practice where you use six images for the instruction.[17] Here Pabongka Rinpoche detailed for us the various points; he said, for example, that he spoke first about how we should avoid the problem of being like a dirty pot because a good motivation was important not only for our classroom hours, but essential too for the steps of contemplation and meditation that should follow the initial period of instruction.

Now there is a great highway along which each and every Buddha of the three times travels. It is the single guiding lamp for living beings in all three lands.[18] It is none other than the teaching known as the "Steps to Buddhahood." And the heart, the very life of this teaching, is the instruction on the three principal paths.

We would all like to become Buddhas so we could help others; but to do so, we have to work to achieve this state. To do this though we have to know how. And to know how, we must study the dharma. The study that we do, moreover, must center on a path that never errs.

This brings us to our present text, the *Three Principal Paths,* which was composed by the protector Gentle Voice as he appeared to his disciples in the form of a man—the great Tsongkapa. He granted the teaching to Ngawang Drakpa, a friar from Tsako district, out to the east in Gyamo Valley.[19] We will offer just a brief account of this profound work, following the words of each verse.

Here we speak of the "three principal paths," while in the teaching on the steps to Buddhahood we talk of practicioners of "three different scopes."[20] Aside from this distinction in the names we give them, and some differences in their section divisions, the teachings on the three principal paths and those on the steps to Buddha-hood are essentially the same. A separate teaching tradition has developed for the present text because of the different categories it employs for the very same subject matter.

The three principal paths are like the main beam that supports all the rest of the roof; your mind must be filled with these three thoughts if you hope to practice any dharma at all, whether it be the open or the secret teachings of the Buddha. A mind caught up in renunciation leads you to freedom, and a mind filled with hopes of becoming a Buddha for the sake of every living being brings you to the state of omniscience. A mind imbued with correct view, finally, serves as the antidote for the cycle of life.

Otherwise you can do non-virtuous deeds, what we call "non-merit," and take a birth in one of the lives of misery.[21] Deeds of "merit" will only lead you to birth as a man, or a pleasure-being of the desire realm. The deeds we call "invariable" will take you as far as a pleasure being of the form or formless realms. You can pretend to practice anything—the Channels and Winds and Drops, the Great Seal, the Great Completion, the Creation and Completion, whatever.[22] But unless the three principal paths fill your thoughts, each of these profound practices can only bring you back to the cycle of birth—they can't even begin to lead you to freedom, or to the state of knowing all.

We find it in the question that Geshe Puchungwa asked of Chen-ngawa:[23] "Let's say on the one hand that you could be one of those people who has mastered all five sciences,[24] who has gained the firmest of single-pointed concentration, someone with each of the five types of clairvoyance,[25] who's experienced all eight of the great attainments.[26] And let's say on the other hand that you could be a person who had yet to gain any full

realization of Lord Atisha's teachings,[27] but who nonetheless had developed such a firm recognition of their
truth that no one else could ever change your mind.
Which of the two would you choose to be?"

And Chen-ngawa spoke in reply, "My master, leave
alone any hope of realizing all the steps to
Buddhahood—I would rather even to be a person who
had just begun to get some glint of understanding, who
could say to himself that he had started off on the first of
these steps to Buddhahood.

"Why would this be my choice? In all my lives to now
I've been a master of the five sciences, countless times.
And countless times I've gained single-pointed concentration, even to where I could sit in meditation for an
eon. The same with the five types of clairvoyance—and
the eight great attainments. But never have I been able
to go beyond the circle of life—never have I risen above
it. If I were able to gain a realization of the steps to
Buddhahood that Atisha taught, I would surely be able
to turn from this round of births."

The same point is conveyed by the stories of the Brahmin's son by the name of Tsanakya,[28] the master meditator of the practice called "Lo Diamond,"[29] and others as
well. The lord Gentle Voice said it to our protector, the
great Tsongkapa:

Suppose you fail to devote some part of your practice to think·
ing over the various problems of cyclic life, and the different
benefits of freedom from it. You don't sit down and meditate,
keeping your mind on trying to open your eyes to the ugliness
of life, or holding it on the wonders of freedom. You don't
reach the point where you never give a thought to the present
life. You never master the art of renunciation.

And let's say you go out then and try to develop a skill in
some great virtuous practice—the perfection of giving, or that
of morality, or forbearance, effort, or staying in concentration.[30] It doesn't matter what. None of it can ever lead you on
to the state of freedom. People who really long for freedom

34

then should forget at first about all those other supposedly so deep advices. They should use the "mental review" meditation to develop renunciation.

People who are trying to practice the greater way should set aside some regular periods of time for consider how harmful it is to concentrate on your own welfare, and how much good can come from concentrating on the welfare of others. Eventually these thoughts can become habitual; nothing that you ever do without them will ever turn to a path that leads you anywhere.

Virtues performed the other way are altered by the fact that you are doing them for yourself—so all they can do in the end is bring you to what is known as a "lower enlightenment." This is similar to what happens when you are unable to practice the various aspects of renunciation deeply because you have failed to devote some time to thinking about it—every virtue you do is affected by your concern for this present life, and only leads you back to the cycle of birth.

It's a definite necessity then first to gain fluency in the attitudes of renunciation and the desire to achieve Buddhahood for every living being; so set aside for the time being all those supposedly profound practices, the secret teachings and so on.

Once you've managed to develop these attitudes, every single virtuous act you perform leads you, despite yourself, to freedom and the state where you know all things. Therefore it's a sign of total ignorance about the very crux of the path when a person doesn't consider these thoughts worth his meditation time.[31]

What we mean above by "mental review" meditation is the type of meditation where you choose a particular line of thought and analyze it. Now the three principal paths are the top of the cream skimmed from all the holy words that the Buddhas have uttered. You see, the meanings of these words and the commentaries upon them have all been packed into the teaching on the paths for practicioners of three different scopes. And this teaching has all been packed further, into the teaching on the steps to Buddhahood. This teaching, in turn, has been packed into that of the three principal paths.

How is each packed into the next? Every single

thought expressed in the holy words of the Buddhas, and in the commentaries which explain them, was uttered for the sole purpose of helping disciples to attain the state of Buddhahood. To achieve this state, one must verse himself in the two causes that bring it about: we call them "method" and "wisdom." The main elements of these two causes are also two: the desire to attain Buddhahood for the sake of all living beings, and correct view. To develop these attitudes in the stream of one's mind, a person must first gain an absolute disgust for all the apparent good things of the life he himself is spending in the circle of births.

Suppose you never manage to develop a desire to get free of the cycle of life yourself—suppose you never reach a renunciation which is complete in every respect. It will be impossible then for you to develop what we call "great compassion"—the desire to liberate every other living being from the cycle. This makes renunciation a "without which, nothing."

Now in order to achieve the Buddha's body of form,[32] a person must first gather together what we refer to as the "collection of merit." This gathering depends principally on the desire to achieve Buddhahood for the sake of every living being. To achieve the Buddha's dharma body, a person must have the "collection of wisdom." Here the most important thing is to develop correct view. All the most vital points of the path then have been packed into the three principal paths, and made into an instruction which can be carried out by students. These words of advice, imparted directly to our precious lord by Gentle Voice himself, are therefore very special indeed.

There's no way to turn your mind to spiritual practice unless you have renunciation from the very first. And there's no way for this practice to serve as a path of the greater way unless you have the desire to become a Buddha for the sake of every living being. And there's no way to rid yourself totally of the two obstacles[33] unless you have correct view. This is why these three attitudes were spoken to be the "three principal paths."

Once you have gained some facility in the three principal paths, everything you do becomes a spiritual practice. If your mind is not filled with these three thoughts, then everything you try leads you nowhere further than the same old circle of births. As the *Greater Steps to Buddhahood* says,

Suppose you try to perform some kind of virtuous deeds, but you have yet to find that special antidote that destroys your tendency to crave for the good things of this circling life—you have yet to succeed in that meditation where you've analyzed all the drawbacks of the circle of life using all the various reasons we've set forth above.

Suppose too that you still haven't been able to investigate the meaning of "no self-nature" as you should, using the analytical type of wisdom. And let's say further that you still lack any familiarity with the two types of desire to reach Buddhahood for every living being.[34]

If you happen to do a few good deeds this way towards some particularly holy object, you might get some good results, but only because of the object's power. Otherwise everything you've done is simply the same old source of suffering—and you come back round around the round of rebirth.[35]

The Seers of the Word in olden days were making the same point when they used to say, "Everybody's got some mystic being they're meditating about and everybody's got some mystic words that they're talking about and all because nobody's got any real practice they're thinking about."[36]

Therefore those of us who are thinking about doing some really pure practice of the spirit should try to find one that will take us on to freedom and all-knowingness. And for a practice to be this way, it should make us masters in the three principal paths. These three are like the heart, the very life within the teachings on the steps to Buddhahood. As the all-knowing Lord, Tsongkapa, once said: "I used the *Lamp on the Path* as my basic text, and made these three the very life of the path."[37]

So now we ourselves will give just a brief teaching using the *Three Principal Paths* — the words of this same Lord Tsongkapa — as our basic text.

III. AN OFFERING OF PRAISE

We'll start by discussing the general outline of the work. This instruction on the three principal paths comes in three basic divisions: the preliminaries that lead into the composition of the text, the main body of the text, and the conclusion of the explanation. The first of these divisions has three sections of its own: an offering of praise, a pledge to compose the work, and then a strong encouragement for the reader to study it well.

What we call the "offering of praise" is contained in the opening line of the work:

I bow to all the high and holy lamas.

The very first thing a person should do when he composes a commentary is to bow to his lord of lords. As Master Dandin said,

> The benediction, bow, and the essence
> Must be written: they are the door.[38]

And we read as well that, "One should bow to the one he holds his lord."

The purpose of this prostration is that one be able to bring his composition to its completion, and that he do so without any interruptions or obstacles. The word "all" in the expression "all the lamas" is meant to refer in a general sense to all of one's immediate and lineage lamas — those who have passed on the teachings through traditions like those known as the "far-reaching activity" and the "profound view."[39] In a very special sense, the word has the meaning that we see it given in the prayer called "Knowledge Unlocks the World": it refers to the victor, Diamond Holder; to the glorious lord, Gentle Voice; and to the Hero of the Diamond.[40]

Now the lord, Gentle Voice, was appearing constantly to the great Tsongkapa. There are different ways such a being can appear to a person: you can see him in a dream, in your imagination, or directly. There are two ways you can see him directly: either with your physical senses, or with your mental sense. The way that Gentle Voice appeared to our protector, the great Tsongkapa, was straight to his physical senses; they sat like teacher and student, and Tsongkapa was able to learn from him every one of the open and secret teachings.

We do see some people who think otherwise: that our Lord Lama was able to write his various treatises merely out of some scholastic skill and moral depth. The truth though is that there is not a single example in all the writings of Lord Tsongkapa—no single treatise, great or small—that was not spoken by Gentle Voice himself. Lord Tsongkapa consulted Gentle Voice in every single thing he did, and followed the instructions he was given—even down to where he should stay, and how many attendants he should take with him when he went somewhere.

This Lord of Lamas was able to make definitive explanations of every deep and vital point in both the open and secret teachings—of things that all the sages gone before had never been able to fathom. These explanations are in no way something that Lord Tsongkapa came up with on his own; they came, rather, from the lips of Gentle Voice himself.

In general it is the custom, when one writes the offering of praise at the beginning of a Buddhist treatise, to express obeisance to compassion, the three types of knowledge,[41] or any other of a great many holy objects. Here though the prostration is made to "the lamas," for a very good reason. The reader wants in general to gain the steps of the path to Buddhahood—and more specifically, the three principal paths—within his own mind. The point of the prostration is to make him realize that this is all going to depend on how well he can follow the practice of proper behavior towards his spiritual teacher.

IV. HOW TO TAKE A LAMA

Now a lama is extremely important at the outset of any attempts at a spiritual life. As Geshe Potowa said,

To reach liberation, there is nothing more important than a lama. Even in simple things of this present life, with things that you can learn just by sitting down and watching someone, you can't get anywhere without a person to show you. So how on earth are you going to get anywhere without a lama, when you want to go somewhere you've never gone before, and you've only just arrived from a journey through the lower births?[42]

Therefore you're absolutely going to have to go and learn from a lama; just reading dharma books is not going to work. There has never been a single person in history who gained his spiritual goals without a lama, just by reading books on dharma. And it will never happen in the future either.

Now what kind of lama should he be? It takes a guide who knows every turn of the path just to get you somewhere you can reach in a single day. For a lama who's supposed to lead you on to freedom and the state of knowing all things, you're going to need one who has all the requisite qualities. It's important to find a really qualified lama; it's not something you shouldn't care much about, because you're going to end up like him—

for better or for worse. The student comes out according to the mold, like those little clay tablets with holy images pressed into them.

What are the characteristics that make a lama qualified? According to the teachings on vowed morality he should be, as they say, a "source of all good qualities" and so on.[43] This means that the lama should possess the two good qualities of being steady and wise.[44] According to the secret teachings, he should fit the description that starts with the words "all three gateways well restrained." According to general tradition—that of both the open and the secret teachings— the lama should have ten fine qualities, as mentioned in the verse that begins with "You who have all ten . . ."

At the very least, your lama must absolutely be a person who has controlled his mind by practicing the three trainings,[45] who possesses a knowledge of the scriptures, and who possesses actual realizations. As the *Jewel of the Sutras* states,

> Take yourself to a spiritual guide controlled,
>   at peace,
> High peace, with exceeding qualities and effort,
>   who's rich
> In scripture, with a deep realization of suchness,
>   a master instructor
> Who's the very image of love, and beyond becoming
>   discouraged.[46]

The prospective disciple on his part should familiarize himself with these descriptions of a proper lama's qualifications, and then seek out a lama who possesses them. Whether the disciple himself turns out to be more or less blessed with virtues depends on the degree to which his lama possesses high personal qualities. If the disciple enjoys a relationship with a lama who is capable of guiding him through the entire range of the open and secret paths, then the disciple will come to be one blessed, in the sense of having heard about and gained some understanding of the paths in their entirety. Even just gaining this general idea of the overall paths represents greater merit that any other good qualities that the student might possess.

Once the disciple does manage to locate a lama with the qualities described above, he must rely on him in the proper way. Here there are eight great benefits a person can gain through proper behavior towards his teacher, beginning with being "close to Buddhahood."[47] There are also eight different dangers of improper behavior towards one's lama—these are the opposites of the benefits just mentioned.

As the great Lord Tsongkapa said himself,

> First then see that the very root for getting
>   an excellent start
> Towards any of the goods things in the present
>   or future lives
> Is effort in proper behavior in both thought
>   and practice towards
> The spiritual guide who shows the path; so
>   please him with the offering
> Of carrying out his every instruction,
>   never giving up
> A single one even when it may cost you
>   your life.
> I, the master meditator, put this
>   into practice;
> You, who seek for freedom, must
>   conduct yourselves this way.[48]

Those of past days, people like Lord Atisha and the great Drom Tonpa,[49] gained matchless levels of realization and were able to perform mighty deeds beyond equal—all of this came because each of them succeeded in maintaining the proper relationship with his own spiritual guide. And it doesn't end there—we can point to Lord Milarepa[50] and others of olden days, and say exactly the same thing.

Proper behavior with one's spiritual guide has tremendous potential—both good and bad—in determining whether a person gets off to an auspicious start in his practice. Marpa slipped before Naropa and ruined his chances for an auspicious beginning.[51] Milarepa offered Marpa a copper pot—empty, but absolutely clean. His start with his practice then was one both good and bad—in exact correspondence to the good and bad of the gift.

The great throneholder Tenpa Rabgye nursed the master tutor Ngawang Chujor most effectively during the latter's illness; as a result, he was able to gain a realization of the "middle view."[52] The Sakya Pandita as well performed perfect service as the nurse of Venerable Drakgyen. Everything that came to him later was because of this service: he was able to see his lama as the deity Gentle Voice; he gained a totally unimpeded knowledge of the five great sciences; a mass of human kind in all the lands of China, Tibet, Mongolia, and elsewhere raised him in honor to the very tip of their heads; and the list goes on and on.[53]

We should speak here too of the dangers in improper behavior towards one's lama. A reference in *Difficult Points to the Black Enemy* puts it this way:

> A person who doesn't treat as a lama
> Someone who's taught him so much as a line
> Will take a hundred births as a dog
> And then be born in the lowest of castes.[54]

The root text of the secret teaching on the Wheel of Time states as well:

> Seconds of anger toward your lama
> Destroy equal eons of virtue collected,

Then bring equal eons in which you endure
The terrible pain of hells and the rest.[55]

Now the length of time in the snap of a finger is itself
made up of no less than sixty-five of what we call
"instants of minimum action." If an emotion of anger
towards your lama comes up in your mind for this period,
for sixty-five of these split-seconds, then you will have to
stay in hell for a period equal to sixty-five *eons*. This by
the way is how the tradition of the lesser way describes it;
according to the teachings of the greater way, the period
is even longer.[56]

And there are even more dangers; a person who
behaves improperly towards his lama will, as the *Fifty
Verses on Lamas* describes, suffer even more in this
present life: spirits, various sicknesses, and other such
problems will harass him constantly. In the hour of
death, he is tormented by excruciating pain at the vital
points and overwhelmed by terror. Moreover, he dies
through one of the thirteen causes of a premature
death — and so on.[57]

There are even further examples of the dangers; we can
recall the master Sangye Yeshe,[58] whose eyes dropped out
of their sockets, or the disciple of Geshe Neusurpa who
met with an untimely death, among others.[59] In short, it
is stated that the result which ripens onto a person in his
future lives once he has spoken ill of his lama is so horri-
ble that even a Buddha would be incapable of describing
it fully. The person takes his rebirth in the lowest of all
hells, known as "Torment Without," where the pain goes
on without stopping.

When we speak of "proper behavior towards your
lama," it's necessary for the student to realize that we
draw no distinction between the person who delivers him
formal dharma teachings and the person who teaches
him the alphabet and so on. Whatever a disciple under-
takes in the service of his lama during the length of their

relationship—whether it be attending to him, paying him respects, or so on, everything except those minor things like the personal daily recitations that the student does for himself—all of it counts as what we call "lama practice." As such it is unnecessary for a disciple in the service of his lama to go out and seek one of the other, formal meditative techniques that are known as "lama practice."

Each of the eight benefits and eight dangers comes up in exact accordance to how well or poorly one behaves with his lama. During the relationship the disciple should use what we call "analytical meditation." To do so, he first has to lay out in his mind each separate point in the teaching on how to behave towards a lama. For example, he could start with the fact that the Holder of the Diamond declared a person's lama to be the Buddha himself.[60] Then the disciple should use various other cases of scriptural authority, together with logical reasoning, to satisfy himself of the truth of each point.

This type of analytical meditation is something that you absolutely can't do without. Despite this fact, here in Tibet the only person to recognize analytical meditation as a form of meditation was Lord Tsongkapa. There is a kind of meditation known as "running" meditation, where you set your mind to run along the concepts related to some words you are reciting. Then there is "reviewing," where you try to recall each point in a particular teaching and think to yourself simply "This one goes like this, and that one goes like that." Analytical meditation is something different; here, you approach each point as something you have to prove or disprove—you set it at center stage in your mind and analyze it using a great number of statements from accepted authorities, and various lines of reasoning.

As a matter of fact, it's "analytical meditation" for example when people like us direct our thoughts over and over to some object that we desire, or something similar. And because of this meditation our desire — or whatever other unhealthy emotion it might be — gets stronger and stronger until we can say we have gained some fluency in it. The idea here is to turn the process around: to perform analytical meditations, one by one, on points such as the fact that the Holder of the Diamond declared that one's lama is the Buddha himself. This way we quickly come to a different type of fluency — in the realization of truth.

The entire concept of how one should take himself to a lama in the proper way is indicated here in the work on the principal paths with these simple words of praise: "I bow to all the high and holy lamas." There is, incidentally, a way you can interpret the words "high," "holy," and "lamas" in the line as referring to persons of the lesser, middle, and greater scopes of practice.

V. A PLEDGE TO COMPOSE THE WORK

Here we have reached the second of the preliminaries that lead into the composition of the text. This is the pledge to compose the text, and is contained in the very first verse:

(1)

As far as I am able I'll explain
The essence of all high teachings of the Victors,
The path that all their holy sons commend,
The entry point for the fortunate seeking freedom.

The principal thing that a person should put to practice — *the essence of all the high teachings of the Victors* — is the three principal paths, or what we call the "Steps of the Path." This teaching on the Steps of the path to Buddhahood is the only one where all the high teachings of the Victors have been combined into a single series of

Steps that any given person can put into practice himself. Such a combination is found in no other separate instruction, open or secret, in any of the traditions, whether we're talking about the three of the Sakya, Geluk, and Nyingma, or any other lineage.[61] We see this in lines such as the one written by Gungtang Jampeyang: "Every high teaching, literal or not, and consistent . . ."[62] The sentiment too is expressed in the epistle that the omniscient Tsongkapa offered to Lama Umapa:

I have come to the realization that only the unerring exposition of the Steps to the paths in both the logical and the secret traditions contained in the work on the Steps of the path to Buddhahood imparted by that great being, the glorious Dipamkara Jnyana, is worthy of such wonder; as such, the steps along which I am presently leading my own disciples I have taken only from it. This teaching of Lord Atisha's appears to me to give the entire contents of the formal commentaries and private instructions on both the words of the Buddha and later explanations of them, by combining everything into a single series of Steps along a path. I feel thus that if people learn to teach it and to study it, and are thereby able to impart and put it into practice, they will (despite the relative brevity of the work) have gone through the entire teachings of the Buddha in their proper order. For this reason I have not found it necessary to use a great number of different texts in my teaching work here.[63]

Thus we can say that, within just a single teaching session devoted to this work on the Steps to the path to Buddhahood, the teacher has taught and the disciples have heard the essence drawn from every single volume of Buddhist teaching that exists on this entire planet.

Now all the teachings of the victorious Buddhas are included into three collections,[64] and all these are included in the teachings on the Steps of the path to Buddhahood for persons of three different scopes. These teachings themselves are included, in their entirety, within even any one of the very briefest works on the Steps of the path. As the gentle protector, Tsongkapa, has described it himself, " . . . an abbreviated abbreviation of the pith of all the Buddhas' words."[65] The great guide Drom Tonpa said as well,

> His wondrous word is all three the collections,
> Advice adorned by teachings of three scopes,
> A gold and jewel rosary of the Seers,
> Meaningful to all who read its beads.[66]

Thus it is that this teaching on the Steps of the path to Buddhahood is far superior to any other teaching of the Buddha that you might choose, for it possesses what we call the "three distinguishing features" and the "four greatnesses."[67] The special qualities mentioned above are found not even in such holy works as the glorious *Secret Collection*,[68] or the classical commentary known as the *Jewel of Realizations*.[69]

A person who develops a good understanding of these Steps to the path reaches a point where he can go to·any one of those *tsatsa* sheds around town where we dispose of old scriptures and images, pick up any scrap of writing that he finds there, and know just where it fits into his lifetime practice. When you go from here to there, meaning from this single teaching on the Steps out to the mass of the Buddhas' other teachings, the Steps are like a magic key that opens a hundred different doors. Going from there to here, the total contents of that mass of teachings has been packed into these Steps.

Having the ability we've just described is, by the way, what we mean when we say someone has "gained an understanding of the teachings in their entirety." Therefore too the expression "master of all the Buddhas' teachings" is not at all meant to refer to somebody who has put together some neither-here-and-neither-there concoction of all the earlier and later systems, and who is trying to practice that. This point we get as well from something that Tuken Dharma Vajra spoke: "Try to mix up all the systems, the earlier and the later, and you end up outside of both."[70]

When we say here that the entire teachings of the Buddha are packed into the Steps of the path, what we mean is that every vital point of the teachings has been expressed through an abbreviated presentation of the topics contained in the three collections of scripture.

Now about the expression "Steps of the Path"; the royal lama Jangchub Uw once made a petition to Lord Atisha, asking for an instruction that would be of special benefit to keep the teachings of the Buddha in the world.[71] Lord Atisha then spoke the *Lamp on the Path to Buddhahood,* which from that time onwards he referred to as the "Steps of the Path"—and thus the expression began to spread. This teaching though is by no means something that Lord Atisha and the great Tsongkapa invented themselves; rather, it is that grand highway along which each and every Buddha has travelled. As the shorter *Sutra on the Perfection of Wisdom* says it,

> It is this perfection, nothing else, which is
>   the path that's shared
> By all the Victors, stay they in the past,
>   the present, or the future.[72]

This by the way is the ultimate origin of the expression "Steps of the Path."

Therefore the teaching on the Steps of the path is one for all Tibet; still though, some people feel no desire to study it, for they hold it to be a private instruction of the Geluk tradition. They are not at fault; it is only because they have insufficient merit from their past deeds that they think this way.

And that's not all; it is in fact by stepping on to this path well-worn by all the Buddhas that one eventually arrives at the very state all Buddhas have found. Otherwise it doesn't make sense that you'd get anywhere except to some weird path or level that no Buddha or any other high being of the past has ever reached. You and I have no need to fear that we might ever make such a blunder, for we have the Steps of the path for our practice. All this we owe to the great kindness of Lord Atisha and Lord Tsongkapa.

People who have hopes of doing some kind of spiritual practice should study an unerring path such as this one. It's not right just to practice anything you can get ahold of, like some stray dog that gobbles down anything he can find. As the gentle protector, the Sakya Pandita, has said:

> Even in some insignificant business
> Over a horse, a gem, or the like,
> You check: ask everyone, consider it well.
> We see people taking pains like this over
> Even the smallest matters of this life.
> Gaining the ultimate goal of all our
> Countless lives depends on dharma,
> Yet we prize any dharma we might come across,
> Not checking if it's good or bad,
> And act like dogs with a scrap of food.[73]

That's just how it is—even in every little matter of this present life, like when you're buying or selling something, you take a lot of care: you do everything you can think of, you run around and ask other people, you spend a lot of time thinking over what to do yourself. But no matter how big a mistake you make with something like this, it's not going to help or hurt you in your future life at all. If you meet up with a spiritual teaching that's wrong though, you make a mistake that affects the ultimate goal of all your lives.

Generally speaking a lot of us go off to some deserted place with the notion that we're going to do some deep practice there. But unless you go with some instruction in hand that is really complete and totally correct, and unless you work to dig down to its core, most of what you do won't be much more than simple wasted effort. As Lord Milarepa once said,

> *The point:* if you don't meditate on advices
>   passed down ear to ear;
> *The place:* you can sit in a mountain cave,
>   but only to torture yourself.[74]

Now the master translators of old undertook a great many hardships, journeying afar to the land of India to bear authentic dharma teachings back here to Tibet. But those in Tibet who followed a mistaken path couldn't live up to them at all. Really good water should at the end of ends trace back to some pure snow. Just so, whatever dharma we choose to practice should have its ultimate origin in something infallible: in the very Lord of the Word, in the Teacher, in the Buddha.

You can spend a thousand years struggling to practice some dharma teaching that has no authentic origin, and you still won't get a single sliver of true realization. It's like thrashing water to make butter.

Therefore we can say that the teaching we decide to practice should have three distinguishing features:

1) It should have been taught by the Buddha.
2) It should have been cleaned of any errors: sages must have brought the teaching to its authentic final form, having examined it to determine whether any wrong ideas crept into it after the Buddha taught it.
3) It should have brought true realizations to the hearts of master practitioners, once they have heard, considered, and meditated upon it. And then it must have passed to

us through the various generations of an
unbroken lineage.

If the dharma we seek to practice has these three characteristics, it is authentic. We from our side still might fail
it, through lapses in our effort and daily practice, but we
need never fear that the teaching from its side will fail
us.

And that authentic teaching is this very Steps to the
path. The highest, the acme, of everything that the Buddha spoke is the precious collection of teachings on the
perfection of wisdom. The overt subject matter of these
teachings consists of the "instructions on the
profound"—on emptiness. These are included in the
Steps within those we call the "profound steps." The
wisdom sutras also present what are known as the "far-
reaching" instructions: those on working to save all living
beings. These points are included in the Steps within
those we call the "far-reaching steps." This then is why
only the teaching on the Steps of the path is one both
complete and free of error. And this is why people who
are looking for a dharma teaching that is worthy of their
practice should most surely begin the Steps.

We see a number of people who out of a mistaken
loyalty to their family traditions stick stubbornly to whatever beliefs their parents happened to have held. They
follow the Bon or some similar mistaken path and in the
end it fails them; the whole great purpose of the present
life they live, and their future lives as well, is carried away
on the wind.

That great accomplished sage, Kyungpo Neljor, was
too a follower of Bon in the beginning.[75] Later on he
realized that Bon had errant beginnings, and so he got
into the earlier secret traditions. These too, he came to
learn, were faulty—so he travelled to India. Here he
studied the later secret traditions and brought his practice to its desired end, gaining the great accomplish-

ments. And there were many others as well—the great Sakya lama Kun-nying, for example—who did the same.[76]

So now we can put the first verse into perspective. Lord Tsongkapa is saying, *"As far as I am able I'll explain the* teaching on the three principal paths. It is that excellent *path that all the Victors' holy sons commend* with their praise, the path on which they travel. It has no error. It goes no mistaken way. It is the highest of all doorways: it is *the entry point for those* people *of* good *fortune* who are *seeking freedom."*

The words "as far as I am able" in the verse are in general put there by Lord Tsongkapa as an expression of modesty. More specifically they have the effect of saying, "As far as I am able I will explain something of as great meaning as can be put into the few words here."

There is another way of glossing the verse, according to which the first line of explanation—the one that includes the words "all high teachings of the Victors"—refers to renunciation. As *Chanting the Names* says,

> The renunciation of all three vehicles
> Lies in the end in a single vehicle.[77]

The point is that the Buddha, in some of his teachings which should be interpreted rather than taken literally, said that there were three different vehicles or ways. These three though are really only one, from the viewpoint of the ultimate end to which they lead. In a similar sense, all the high teachings of the Victors were enunciated as a means to produce the ultimate "renunciation"—the Buddha's knowledge—within the minds of disciples. And renunciation is what, at the very beginning, urges one to develop a disgust for the cycle of life and set his mind on reaching freedom. This is why the attitude of renunciation is taught here first, in the first line.

The second line of explanation—the one that includes the words "their holy sons"—refers to the wish to achieve enlightenment for every living being. This is the attitude that all the Victors and their sons take as their single most important meditation, and the attitude whose praises they sing. It is like a great center beam that holds up the entire structure of the greater way.

The third line of explanation—the one with the words "the fortunate seeking freedom"—refers to correct view. This perception is the one and only entry point for disciples who seek for freedom. To achieve freedom, you have to cut ignorance—the root of this circle of life. And to cut ignorance, you have to develop the wisdom which realizes no-self. And to develop wisdom, you need a correct view free of all error.

Correct view is the single door to nirvana, to peace. And so it is that the great Tsongkapa, in the closing words of the verse, pledges to compose his work on the three principal paths—which include correct view. His pledge is made in the way prescribed by Master Dandin:[78] he abbreviates within it all the topics to be treated in the work itself—which here would be to say he includes within his pledge every *essential* point in the entire body of the paths to be explained. In this sense, our Lama concluded, Lord Tsongkapa had in the first verse already taught us the essence of the paths.

VI. ENCOURAGEMENT TO STUDY

We have now reached the third and final of the preliminaries that lead into the composition of the text. This one consists of a strong encouragement for the reader to study the work well, and is contained in the next verse of the root text:

(2)

Listen with a pure mind, fortunate ones
Who have no craving for the pleasures of life,
And who to make leisure and fortune meaningful strive
To turn their minds to the path which pleases
 the Victors.

Here the great Tsongkapa is urging his readers to study the work: "You, you people *who* are seeking freedom and *have no* single moment's *craving for the pleasures of life;* you, who want to get the absolute most from the body you've found, *to make* your *leisure and fortune meaningful;* you now are going to have to train yourself in a path that never errs, a path that never strays, a path that is whole and complete, *the path which pleases* even *the Buddhas*—the one in the end they advise, a path that is no erring path, a path that is no path that strays, a path that is more than just some piece or part of a path. And if you want to train yourself in a path like that, you're going to have to be a student who has all the requirements of a student; you're going to have to fit the description from the *400 Verses:*

We call someone a proper vessel for study
Who's unbiased, intelligent, and willing to strive.[79]

And *fortunate ones* like you, disciples who have *turned their minds* to the dharma, are going to have to *listen with a pure mind;* avoid in your study those things which are opposed to its success—the three problems of the pot; rely in your study on those things which are conducive to its success—the six images for the instruction."[80]

There is another way of interpreting the verse which says we should regard the line about those "who have no craving for the pleasures of life" as referring to renunciation—the first of the three principal paths. The next line, the one about making your "leisure and fortune meaningful," applies then to the wish to achieve enlightenment for all living beings, because anyone who's trained his mind in this attitude has certainly gotten the absolute most from his life of leisure and fortune. And the final line, the one about the "path which pleases Victors," relates to correct view since, as the root text itself states later on,

> A person's entered the path that pleases the Buddhas
> When for all objects, in the cycle or beyond,
> He sees that cause and effect can never fail,
> And when for him they lose all solid appearance.

This then completes our presentation of the customary preliminaries: the offering of praise, pledge to compose the work, and encouragement for the reader to study it well. We can relate what we've said so far to the opening sections of works such as the greater and medium-length presentations of the complete Steps to Buddhahood. The line that reads "I bow to all the high and holy lamas" relates to the first section in these works, known as "demonstrating the eminence of the author in order to show that the teaching comes from an authentic source." The lines from "As far as I am able . . ." up to " . . . seeking freedom" correspond to the second section, on the "eminence of the teaching." The verse that goes from "Listen with a pure mind . . ." up to " . . . path which pleases the Victors" gives us the third section, which is "how to study and teach" the Steps. The last great section of these presentations is known as "the instruction itself, by which students can be led along the Steps" to Buddhahood. This part is contained in what we have called here the "main body of the text" of Lord Tsongkapa's verses on the three principal paths. Thus we now move on to the first one of these verses.[81]

THE FIRST PATH:
RENUNCIATION

VII. WHY YOU NEED RENUNCIATION

OUR TREATMENT OF the main body of the text will break down into four parts: an explanation of renunciation, an explanation of the wish to achieve enlightenment for every living being, an explanation of correct view, and some strong words of encouragement—that the reader should try to recognize the truth of these instructions and actually go and practice them. The explanation of renunciation itself will proceed in three sections: reasons why one should try to develop it, how one goes about developing it, and the point at which we can say one has succeeded in developing it. The first of these sections is found in the next verse of Lord Tsongkapa's work:

(3)

There's no way to end, without pure renunciation,
This striving for pleasant results in the ocean of life.
It's because of their hankering life as well that beings
Are fettered, so seek renunciation first.

Now for all of us to escape from the cycle of life, we have to want to escape. If we never develop the wish to get out, and we get attached to the good things of this circle of life, then there will never be any way to escape it.

A prisoner can sit in a jail, but if he never really wants to escape, and never really attempts an escape, he never will escape. It's the same for us—if we never try to find some way to escape this cycle of life, the day of our escape will never arrive. If we work to develop the wish to escape, then surely there will come a time when we do.

Here first we have to understand just how we spin around in this life-circle. The "cycle of life" is defined as taking on, again and again, the impure groups of things that make up a normal suffering being—it is their unbroken stream from life to life.[82] What is it that chains us to this cycle? Our own deeds and bad thoughts. And to what exactly are we chained? To those impure parts of our being.

To get free of this cycle of life we must recognize that everything about it is, by nature, complete suffering. This brings a disgust for it, a loathing for it, and this then brings renunciation for it. Thus what the verse is saying is: *"Without pure renunciation, there's no way to stop this* attitude where one *strives* for whatever *pleasant results* he might get here *in life. Moreover, it is* precisely *by force of their* feelings of attachment and craving for the pleasant things of *life* (here *'hankering'* is another name for what we usually refer to as 'craving'), *that* all *beings are fettered.* And if all beings are fettered, do you imagine that you are not? Of course you are. If you want some day to escape this cycle, *seek then*, at the very *first*, a pure attitude of *renunciation."*

This verse by the way incorporates what the works on the Steps to Buddhahood refer to as the "instructions for those of lesser and of medium scope." We see some people around with the notion that to reach enlightenment you only need to practice the wish to achieve Buddhahood for all living beings—that you don't need to practice renunciation. The truth though is that, even just to reach a lower nirvana,[83] renunciation is an absolute necessity; in fact, it has to be *fierce* renunciation. As the great Tsongkapa, our Protector, has said himself:

About this attitude—it's just the way Sharawa described it. Suppose it's no stronger in your heart than a thin film of barley powder spread out on the surface of some homemade beer. Then your feeling that you want to avoid the cause of the cycle of life—what we call the "origin"—will be no stronger than that. Then your aspiration to reach nirvana, where you stop both suffering and its origin, will be exactly the same way. And then your wish to practice the path that brings this nirvana will be nothing but empty words. So too for compassion, the state of mind where you can no longer bear to see other living beings wander through the cycle: there's no way you will gain it. Then finally you will never find a genuine form of the wish to achieve matchless enlightenment for all living beings, a powerful wish that can urge you on. And so the "greater way" becomes for you nothing but some flimsy understanding of the descriptions you find of it in books.[84]

The point here is that, to develop the wish to achieve enlightenment for all living beings, you must first develop a kind of compassion where you can no longer bear to see these beings tormented by the sufferings of life. To develop this, you must develop renunciation over your own situation; there is no way otherwise you could gain compassion, for it contemplates the situation that others must face. This too, concluded our Lama, is what Lord Atisha meant in his gentle rebuke to us Tibetans: "Only in Tibet have they found people with the wish for enlightenment who haven't yet found love and compassion."[85]

VIII. STOPPING DESIRE FOR THIS LIFE

This brings us to the second section of our explanation of renunciation; that is, a description of how to develop it. First we'll talk about how to stop desire for the present life, and then how to stop it for future lives. Stopping desire for this life is the subject of the next two lines of the root text:

(4a)

Leisure and fortune are hard to find, life's not long;
Think it constantly, stop desire for this life.

What we mean by "desire for this life" is this desire for happiness and fame in this life—where you say to yourself, "If only I could get more of the good things of life than anyone in the world—the best food, finest clothes, biggest name, and all the rest." Anyone who hopes to do some spiritual practice must stop his desire for this life.

How to stop it? You must contemplate the two Steps known as (1) the "great importance of this life of leisure and fortune, and the difficulty of finding it," as well as (2) our "impermanence, the fact that we must die." These thoughts then will turn back your desire for this life—in your mind, you will give up on it. The fact that you and I right now never do any spiritual practice—no, worse, the fact that we try and what we do is anything but spiritual practice—is all because of our desire for this life. *Free of Four Loves,* the mental-training text, puts it this way:

> No practitioner, a person who loves this life.
> No renunciation, a mind that loves the cycle.[86]

The border that separates spiritual practice from what is not, and the border that separates real spiritual practice from what is not, is this attitude of having given up on this life. Practice, in the form of reciting some lines, and the world may somewhere meet; but there is no way that practice in the form of giving up on this life will ever meet the world, in the form of happily participating in this life. There is no way you can keep the world, and still keep your practice.

This is what the precious preceptor, Drom Tonpa, had in mind when he said to a certain monk, "It makes my heart glad, uncle, to see you walking round this holy place to pay your respects; how much gladder would I be, if you did something spiritual!" And he went on to say the same thing about making prostrations, and reciting prayers, and meditating, and everything else. So finally the monk couldn't decide at all what was supposed to be spiritual practice and he asked Drom Tonpa, "Well then, how am I supposed to practice?" And the only answer he got was "Give up on this life!"—repeated three times, and loud.[87]

Then there was the Seer geshe by the name of Shang Nachung Tonpa, who once said,

I go to Lord Atisha and ask him for teaching. But all he says to me is some little sentence like "Give up on this life," or "Practice love," "Practice compassion," or "Practice the wish to achieve enlightenment for all living beings."

Lord Drom Tonpa overheard this complaint, and remarked that "It's amazing. He's just been granted the absolute essence of all Lord Atisha's instruction, yet even someone so great as Shang doesn't comprehend what it is to have a teaching." And later on in his life, Shang would also say to his students that "If you want to practice the spiritual life, the most important thing you can do is give up on this life."[88]

In a broad sense we can start with what are known as the "eight worldly thoughts." These then can be shortened into three concerns of this life: food, clothes, and a big name. These three are what you have to give up on.

The worst of the three by the way is Big Name. Sages, holy men, great meditators of the past—even we can say a majority of them—have been able to live without great food, keeping themselves alive on one of those mystical practices where all you eat is some tiny pills or the essence of a flower. And they've been able to live without great clothes too: they sit in deep retreat, wearing tattered robes covered with dirt—they glue their backs to the wall of a cave and seal the only entrance. But in the bottom of their hearts they still crave fame—the Big Name—and they dream that all the local people outside are talking about what a holy master meditator they are.

There have been many, many sages and scholars and monks who were pure in their moral lives but misled in this same way. As the great Droway Gonpo has said,

> They go into seclusion, post a sign on the door,
> See not a soul, these master contemplators who still
> Hope in this life they call me the "Great Meditator."[89]

As well as,

> And so they fill their minds with hopes and plans,
> Thoughts that come in everything they do,
> And so their spiritual practice goes to waste,
> Spirited away by bandit locals.
> Take a spear then, strike it into every
> Thought that comes for this life, and remember
> Should a single spear not hit the mark
> Being a sage, saint, scholar, meditator
> Cannot close the door to the three lower realms.

The great Ngaripa too has said,

All the spiritual practice you've done has turned into some ambition for eminence in this life. This then turns into what we call the "origin"—a cause for more of the cycle; it increases in you your feelings of pride, and jealousy, dislike for some things and longing for others. Then what you thought was spiritual practice actually takes you to the three lower realms. It's no different than if you'd gone there by doing bad deeds.[90]

Therefore if we want to do any spiritual practice we must quell the eight worldly thoughts—we must stand neutral, free of both members of each of its four pairs. "Eight worldly thoughts" is a name we give to the following eight emotions:

1) Being happy when we acquire some thing,
2) And unhappy when we don't.
3) Being happy when we feel good,

4) And unhappy when we don't.
5) Being happy when we become well known,
6) And unhappy when we don't.
7) Being happy when someone speaks well of us,
8) And unhappy when someone speaks ill of us.

As the *Letter to a Friend* states,

> Oh worldly wise! To gain or not, feel good
> Or not, be well-known or not, be spoken of
> Well or ill, these are the eight worldly thoughts.
> Quell them; let them not come to your mind.[91]

The great saint Lingrepa has said as well,

> In the city of daily concerns in our circle of life
> Scurry the waked cadavers of eight worldly thoughts.
> This is where you can find the most frightening
>   cemetery of all;
> This is where you lamas should keep your midnight
>   vigil among the dead.[92]

It doesn't matter who you are—some great sage, or saint, or master, or meditator—and no matter how profound the practice you imagine you are doing, it is all a hollow sham if it's mixed up with the eight worldly thoughts. We find this truth in the words of Yang Gonpa, a disciple of the victorious Gu-tsangpa:

It doesn't do any good that the teaching is the holy and secret "Great Completion." The person himself has to become holy and secret, great complete. We see a whole pack of cases where the way a person describes his spiritual practice, it would buy a whole herd of horses—but the person himself isn't worth a dog. Religion that's all words and never gets put into daily practice is all the same as some talk a parrot's been taught to squawk; the person and the practice are miles apart; his mind and his religion never quite mix into one, there's lumps of flour that never dissolve in the batter. Babbling on about spiritual practice and never letting it sink in, leaving it to bob around on the surface like some uncooperative vegetables in a soup, is missing the whole point of spiritual practice. I tell you all, what I teach as the crux of all practice is to give up on this life.[93]

Therefore if a person fails to stand free of the eight worldly thoughts for this life he will find it hard even to shut the doors to a birth in the realms of misery, much less do something that's a spiritual practice. To do such a practice, you must take up the instruction called the "Ten Ultimate Riches"—a teaching of the masters called the Seers of the Word for quelling the eight worldly thoughts, and giving up on life. These ten "ultimate riches" are the following:[94]

> The Four Aims.
> The Three Diamonds.
> The Three of Being Thrown Out,
>   and Reaching, and Attaining.

The "four aims" are,

> Aiming your mind ultimately to practice.
> Aiming your practice ultimately to the beggar.
> Aiming the beggar ultimately to death.
> Aiming death ultimately to some dusty ravine.

And the "three diamonds" are,

> Sending the uncatchable diamond ahead of you.
> Laying the unabashable diamond behind you.
> Keeping the wisdom diamond at your side.

The three of "being thrown out, and reaching, and attaining," are, lastly,

> Being thrown out from the ranks of men.
> Reaching the ranks of dogs.
> Attaining the ranks of the gods.

"Aiming your mind ultimately to practice" means to practice religion with the following thoughts: This time I've been able to obtain a good human body and circumstances; they are extremely hard to find, they are incredibly valuable, and they include all the necessary leisure and fortune. This is the one and only time I will have such a life. And it will not be here long; it is absolutely sure that I will die, I have no way of knowing when my death will come. And when I die, only this holy spiritual practice will be of any use to me. All the things and honors I have gathered in this life, every bit of fame I've gained, everything else of the money and possessions I may have with me, will not be the slightest help to me.

"Aiming your practice ultimately to the beggar" is like this: Suppose you think to yourself "But well now, if I stop trying to do what it takes to live well in this life so I can do my spiritual practice, I'm afraid that I won't even find the bare necessities for doing the practice: I'll become a beggar." Think then to yourself this way: "I will undertake any hardship for my practice; and if it means I have to become a mere beggar, then let me become a beggar. I will find a way to do my practice, even if I have to live on lousy scraps of food that I beg off others, and wear any old clothes they give me."

"Aiming the beggar ultimately to death" means never giving up on your practice. Suppose you think to yourself, "So I try to do some practice, and I turn into a beggar, because I haven't taken the time to collect even the single smallest material thing. But then I won't even have what it takes to sustain this human life. I'm afraid some day I'll die, without enough food, without enough clothes." But instead you should think this way: "In all my many previous lives, I've never given up my life for the sake of my practice. If I can die this one time trying to practice, I might make up for it. And anyway we are all the same: rich or poor, we all are going to die. Rich people, to get rich, have collected a lot of bad deeds and

will die with them. I, on the other hand, will accomplish something of very great meaning if I die from the hardships of trying to practice. So if for my practice I freeze to death, let me freeze. If for this I starve, let me starve."

"Aiming your death ultimately to some dusty ravine" comes like his: Suppose you think to yourself, "But there are certain things that I need from now up to the time I die. If I don't have any money at all, how am I going to get someone to help me when I'm sick? Who will attend me in my old age? Who will be there at my deathbed? And who will take care of things after I die—who will take the body away, and all the rest?" All these kinds of thoughts come under the category of attachment to the good things of this life. There's no way at all you can be sure that you'll even live long enough to reach any old age. Better to go to some lonely mountain retreat, and give up attachment to anything at all, and think to yourself "Now I'm going to practice, and I don't care if I die like some stray dog in a dusty ravine, with no one to look after me, and maggots crawling all over the corpse."

"Sending the uncatchable diamond ahead of you" has this meaning: You may be able to give up on life as described above, and start to try your practice. But then your parents and other family, your friends and all the rest will try to catch you and bring you back. Make yourself uncatchable; keep your mind as firm and unchanging as a diamond, even if you have to leave behind your most beloved family and friends, those close to you as the heart in your breast, standing with tears in their eyes from the pain. Leave, go to some lonely mountain hermitage, without any regrets, without any attachments. Stay there and devote yourself to the purest of practice.

"Laying the unabashable diamond behind you" looks like this: Suppose you do give up on this life, and leave. People will despise you, and condemn you, and say things like "Now he's nothing but a useless wandering beggar." But whatever they say you must give up on all of

it, and think to yourself, "If they say I'm as pure as a god, that's fine. If they say I'm as evil as a devil, that's fine too. It doesn't make any difference to me. Trying to keep up a good image with friends who are all devoted to this life can lead to a great many problems, and acts as a great obstacle to spiritual practice."

"Keeping the wisdom diamond at your side" means never transgressing the pledge you have made to yourself. Abandon, and abandon forever, all the absolutely meaningless actions you do out of desire for this life. Keep your mind in the spiritual, firmly, and make your life and your practice one and the same.

"Being thrown out from the ranks of men" comes like this: Now you will start to see that desiring the good things of this present life is your real enemy. Your whole outlook then will start to clash with the outlook that other men have, men high or low, who all nonetheless strive for this life's happiness. To them you are acting like a madman, and so you will be thrown out from the ranks of men—men who live for this life.

"Reaching the ranks of dogs" means that you live your life without any great food, or clothes, or reputation. For the sake of your practice, you endure whatever comes to you in the way of hunger, or thirst, or tiredness.

"Attaining the ranks of the gods" starts with going to some secluded place, and giving up on all the normal activities of the world. You bring your practice to its desired end, and within this very life attain the state of a Buddha—the very god of gods.

By the way, you need never fear that if you give up on things to practice the way we've described it above you'll become some poor beggar and starve to death. It is possible for a worldly person to die of hunger, but absolutely impossible for a religious practitioner to do so. This is because our compassionate Teacher, when he reached the state of total enlightenment, still had merit enough from his past deeds to go and take some 60,000 births as a

69

"Wheel Emperor"—one of those incredibly powerful beings who rule the entire world. Instead he took the fantastic power of these deeds and dedicated it to the food and other necessities that all his future followers might require. In the *White Lotus, the Sutra on Compassion,* we hear the following oath from the Buddha as he first commits himself to reaching enlightenment for the sake of living kind:

And in the days when my teachings spread in the world, any man who wears so much as four inches of the saffron robe shall find food and drink to his heart's desire. If he does not, then I shall have cheated the state of Buddhahood. And then may I lose my Buddhahood.[95]

The Buddha also says,

In future days, there will come in the world a time of famine, when men must pay a box of pearls to buy a box of flour. Not even in such days will a follower of the Teacher ever want for life's necessities.[96]

And finally Lord Buddha has stated,

> Householders, each and every one,
> May plow their crops on a fingernail,
> But those who've left their homes for me
> Will never want for necessities.

These quotations are taken from the collection of sutras and the like; they are the words of a being who cannot lie, and whose words can never fail.

Now when we say to "give up on this life," the main thing that you have to give up is those eight worldly thoughts or attachments, towards the pleasures of this life. Giving up these thoughts doesn't necessarily mean that you have to throw away all your material possessions and become a beggar. Holy teachers of the past have pointed out for us examples of people who succeeded in giving up on life, and these have included personages of fantastic material wealth such as Gyalchok Kelsang Gyatso and the Panchen Lobsang Yeshe.[97]

Then too there is our own Teacher, the compassionate Buddha, who could have had the kingdom of a World Emperor, but gave it up and left the home life. The princes Shantideva and the Great Lord, the glorious Atisha, also relinquished their thrones and left the home.[98] The mighty Lord Tsongkapa as well, acting on the instructions of Gentle Voice, left behind close to a thousand learned students with tears in their eyes, and everything else he had, to go into isolation with but a few hand-picked disciples: the followers known as the "Purest Eight." The Emperor of China in those days even dispatched a letter with his golden seal, carried forth by a Tashin and other high officials, inviting Lord Tsongkapa to the imperial court—but could not induce him to come.[99]

These high beings lived only off their own asceticism and whatever food someone might offer them. They spent their days striving to perfect their practice, and in such activities led a way of life that followed the real meaning of the Ten Ultimate Riches—the teaching of Lord Atisha and the Seers of the Word.

Many are the holy songs of experience from those who have given up this life. The great victor Wensapa, who achieved Buddhahood in this one human life, in this one man's body, spoke the following:

> Milarepa, of days gone by,
> And Lobsang Dundrup in our times
> Had no need for keeping a single thing
> Beyond today's food and the clothes they wore.
> Make the most of your leisure and fortune:
> In isolation, from like and dislike;

> Live life well, follow this way,
> Reach enlightenment in this one life.[100]

The great master of all master meditators, Milarepa, has said as well:

> If in your heart you wish to keep the holy
>   practice, son,
> Within the very depths of it then find
>   this thing first—faith,
> Never turn and look back once again
>   upon—this life.
> If in truth you'll follow after me,
> Your loved ones turn to demons, hold you back;
> Do not think them true—cut all the ties.
> Food and money are the demons' advance guard;
> The closer the worse, give up all want for them.
> The objects of the senses are the demons' snare;
> "They will entrap me!" stop your craving them.
> Your young love is the daughter of the demons;
> "She will mislead me!" so be on your guard.
> The place you grew up is the demons' prison;
> Hard to free yourself from, flee it quick.
> You will have to leave it all behind and
>   go on—later,
> Why not make it meaningful and leave it
>   all—right now?
> It will fall down one day anyway, this
>   mannequin apparition;
> Better to use this body now, get off to a
>   good quick start.
> This skittish bird of mind will anyway fly
>   from the corpse one day;
> Better now to soar across some wide
>   expanse of sky.
> If you listen and act upon this one man's
>   words—of mine,
> Then the grace to keep the holy practice,
>   my boy—is yours.[101]

He said too,

> No way my loved ones know I'm glad,
> No way my enemies know I'm sad;
> If I can die here in this cave
> My hermit's wishes have come true.

> No way my friends know I've got old,
> No way my sister knows I'm sick;
> If I can die here in this cave
> My hermit's wishes have come true.

> No way that people know I've died,
> No rotting corpse that vultures spy;
> If I can die here in this cave
> My hermit's wishes have come true.

> Flies will suck my meat and bones,
> Maggots eat tendons, ligament;
> If I can die here in this cave
> My hermit's wishes have come true.

> No footprints leading from my door,
> No bloodstains left here on the floor;
> If I can die here in this cave
> My hermit's wishes have come true.

> No one to hold a deathbed vigil,
> No one to weep when I am gone;
> If I can die here in this cave
> My hermit's wishes have come true.

> No one to wonder where I went
> No one who knows where I am found;
> If I can die here in this cave
> My hermit's wishes have come true.

> May this death prayer of a beggar
> In the wild of a mountain cave

73

Come to help all living beings;
Then my wishes have come true. [102]

Now there is one instruction which we can call the very
essence of all the teachings on how to get rid of the eight
worldly thoughts of this life. This is the meditation on
one's own impermanence and death. People like us
though must prepare our minds for this meditation by
first contemplating how valuable, and how hard to find,
our present life of leisure and fortune is. Then gradually
we will be ripe for the realization of death.

The all-knowing Lord Tsongkapa has said himself,

> This body of leisure's more valuable than
>   a jewel that gives any wish,
> And now is the only time you will ever
>   find a one like this.
> It's hard to find, and easily dies,
>   like lightning in the sky.
> Think this over carefully, and come
>   to realize
> That every action of the world is like
>   the chaff of grain,
> And so you must strive night and day
>   to make the most of life.
> I, the master meditator, put this
>   into practice;
> You, who seek for freedom, must
>   conduct yourselves this way. [103]

The point here is that, to rid yourself of the eight worldly
thoughts and undertake a spiritual practice which is truly
pure, you must gain two different realizations: first, of
how valuable and hard to find one's life of leisure and
fortune is; secondly, of one's own impermanence and the
fact that he must die. Once you gain these realizations, it
doesn't matter—the hills can turn to gold, the rivers into
milk, and every man your slave—but to you it's all repul-

74

sive, useless, like a feast set before a sick man vomiting. And it's not enough for these realizations to come to you just from the outside—from sitting and listening to someone describe them. They must come from the inside, from thinking about them yourself. Then they will be firm in your mind, and never change again.

Now a single expression in the root verse, the one that reads "Leisure and fortune are hard to find," serves to introduce three different concepts: recognizing one's leisure and fortune, contemplating their incredible value, and contemplating how hard they are to find. What we mean by "leisure" is to be free of the eight different ways a person can lack opportunity, and to the opportunity to attempt some spiritual practice.[104] "Fortune" refers to the fact that one is fortunate enough to possess all the inner and outer circumstances that will allow him to undertake his practice. These include having taken birth as a human being, having entered the Buddha's teaching, and so on.[105]

This body we live in gives us in our own two hands the ability to achieve everything from good things in our next life on up to the state of Buddhahood itself, and thus is incredibly valuable. Such a body and life are difficult to find, from three different points of view.

We can start with the "causal" viewpoint. This life of leisure and fortune is hard to find because it is a specific result of the special causes that can bring one leisure and fortune, and these causes are extremely rare—keeping your moral life completely pure, and so on. Then there is the viewpoint of the "nature of the thing." Generally speaking, there are fewer beings in the happier realms than there are in the realms of misery.[106] Of all those in the happier realms, humans are the fewest. Of all the different human beings, those who live in the world we know are the fewest. And of all the humans in our world, those who've attained leisure and fortune are very, very few. Thus this life's by nature hard to find.

Finally a life like ours is hard to find from the view-point of the "classical example." Suppose there were a single yoke-like ring of pure gold that could float upon the surface of the great ocean. The swells of the sea push it back and forth, in every direction you can imagine. Far down in the very depths of the ocean lives a great sea-turtle. He is sightless. Once, and only once, in the span of an entire century he swims to the surface, to poke his head up momentarily. And suppose the golden ring happens to catch him around the neck. The odds against it are nearly infinite.

Our case is the same. The teachings of the Buddha pass now and again among the various planets of the universe. Here are we, blinded by our ignorance. We are perma-nent inhabitants of the deepest reaches within the ocean of cyclic life. A human body, complete with leisure and fortune, will be fantastically hard to find; the odds against it are almost infinite. But this time we have found one.

So our life of leisure and fortune is incredibly valuable, and difficult to find; this is the first and last time we will ever have such a chance. We must now make the greatest use we can of it. The single highest thing we can do with this life is to practice the Greater Way.

And we must begin this practice now, right now. Little time remains before the inevitable death comes to us. We must constantly bring our death to mind; just some vague awareness that someday death will come, or think-ing some about death, is not enough to really keep your coming death in mind. You must train yourself, meticu-lously, in what it is to die.

In our root text, the instruction on how to keep your mind on death is presented in the words "life's not long." This instruction includes a number of categories: the benefits that come from keeping your mind on death, the problems that come from not keeping your mind on death, and how then actually to keep your mind on death. This last category itself includes the three basic principles, the nine reasons for them, and the three resolves to be made because of them—all ending with the meditation on what it's like to die.[107] A person who trains himself in these categories over a long period of time is able to develop the true attitude of keeping his mind on death, and then gains the ability to turn back his desire for the pleasures of the present life. When a person through the process of careful contemplation has developed this attitude of keeping his mind on his own death and impermanence, then we can say the virtuous way has taken its root within him.

At this point one should study the more detailed presentation of death meditation that appears in the standard works on the Steps of the path to Buddhahood. This applies as well to other topics following, such as how to go for refuge, and the teaching on actions and their consequences. Here in this text, concluded our Lama, the traditional contemplations on the sufferings of the lower births and the entire set of instructions about going for refuge are conveyed by implication, though not directly in the actual words of the verses.

IX. STOPPING DESIRE FOR FUTURE LIVES

This brings us to the teaching on how to stop desire for one's future lives, which is the second step in developing the path known as renunciation.

(4b)

> Think over and over how deeds and their fruits
> never fail,
> And the cycle's suffering: stop desire
> for the future.

Now what we mean by "desire for the future" is the kind of attitude where you think to yourself, "I hope in my future births I can live like some god-like being, such as the creatures they call Pure-One and Hundred-Gift, or like one of those Wheel Emperors who rule the entire world. May I live in some wonderful state of happiness, in the best of places, with the best of things, with a beautiful body and everything I wish for at my fingertips." Incidentally, we also see people who pray to be born in one of the truly pure realms of a Buddha, where they will never have to suffer and can enjoy everlasting happiness—but they pray so without any intention of reaching this high state in order to help other beings. If we really follow this line of thinking to its end, it would appear that people like this have for the most part simply slipped into the base desire for future lives.

In standard texts on the Steps of the path to Buddhahood, we are taught the principles of actions and their consequences in the section for people whose practice is of a lesser scope, in order to stop our desire for this present life. The instructions for people of a medium scope then are meant to help us stop our desire for a future life. Here in the teaching on the three principal paths though we are advised to meditate on our leisure and fortune, as well as impermanence, in order to stop our desire for this life; our desire for future lives is to be stopped by a combination of understanding the principles of actions and their consequences and contemplating the various sufferings of cyclic life.

This latter way of making the presentation is meant to convey two important points. The first is that, since the forces of action and consequence are so extremely subtle, the consequences of any misdeed will wheel one back into the circle of life if one fails to make a complete escape from the cycle first. The second is that, in order to defeat this circle, one must stop each and every action he performs which is motivated by ignorance.

Thus we can say that, in order to escape the circle of life, one must take up white actions and abandon black actions. But to do this, he must believe in the law of actions and consequences at all. And to do this, he must contemplate upon actions and consequences.

This contemplation is done by considering, very carefully, the four principles of action which the Buddha enunciated:

1. Actions are certain to produce similar consequences.
2. The consequences are greater than the actions.
3. One cannot meet a consequence if he has not committed an action.
4. Once an action is committed, the consequence cannot be lost.

Once a person has gained a well-founded belief in these principles, he will automatically in his daily life avoid doing wrong things and begin doing right things.

In texts on the Steps of the path to Buddhahood, the instruction on impermanence is followed by sections that treat the three lower births and how to go for refuge. Here we will weave in some of these points from the Steps—which is also the intent of the text at hand.

After you die, your consciousness doesn't just go out like a lamp—you must take another birth. And there are only two kinds of birth you can take: one of the births of misery, or one of the happier births. As for which of the two you do take, you are totally helpless: you must follow the direction of your past actions. Virtuous actions throw you into one of the happier types of birth, and non-virtuous actions throw you into one of the three of misery.

Great non-virtuous acts lead you to the hells; medium ones lead you to a birth as an insatiable spirit; and lesser non-virtues make you take birth as an animal. Great virtuous acts, on the other hand, bring you a birth as a pleasure-being in one of the two higher realms; medium virtues make you a pleasure being of the desire realm; and lesser virtues bring birth as a human in the same realm.[108] As our glorious protector, Nagarjuna, has stated,

> Non-virtue brings all sufferings
> And all the births of misery.
> Virtue brings all happier births,
> And happiness in all one's births.[109]

Since this is the case, and since all the virtues you and I have are feeble—while all our non-virtues are ever so mighty—then if we were to die in our present condition it's a foregone conclusion that we would take birth in one of the realms of misery.

Taking our birth in one of these realms, we would meet unbearable sufferings. As a hell-being there would be unspeakable heat or cold, our bodies boiled or scorched, and more. As insatiable spirits we would always be hungry, or thirsty, in a constant state of exhaustion and fear. As animals we would be mindless brutes incapable of saying a thing, exploited by humans for their work or food.

There is a way to avoid these births of misery, and this is to turn ourselves over to the three rare jewels[110] for their protection, and do so from the bottom of our hearts, and strive our best in choosing correctly which actions we should undertake, and which we should abandon.

This correct decision in choosing our actions is actually the single most important instruction in the entire teaching on how to go for refuge. Once we disregard the principles of action and consequence, it's already decided that we will take our birth in the realms of misery. People like you and I here in this assembly, mostly monks, are not likely to take one of these lower births simply because we know nothing of the spiritual teachings. But remember: there have been absolute multitudes of people like us, who had a knowledge of the teachings, but who passed to the realms of misery because they could not put these teachings into actual practice, or because they chose to disregard the laws of action and consequence.

And we must heed these laws. A man who does not must take a lower birth, and it doesn't matter how knowledgeable he was, or how saintly. You can be a sage who has mastered the entire contents of the canon, you can be an advanced meditator with fantastic spiritual accomplishments, you can have great extra-sensory powers, and ability to perform miracles; but if you cannot behave with care around action and consequence, you will suffer.

We have for example the monk named Lekkar, who could sit and recite all twelve of the great collections of scripture,[111] as well as Devadatta—who had in his memory no less than that vast amount of scriptures we call a "heap."[112] And yet ultimately it was no use to either one, for they took their rebirth in the hells. This again would seem to be a case where the person had a knowledge of the teachings, but was unable to put them into actual practice, or disregarded the principles of actions and their consequences, or never gained any belief in these principles in the first place. Accounts like these of people who lived before us and made the same mistake are almost countless—and we should learn from them.

So this brings us to the four most general principles in our contemplation of actions and their consequences:

1) If the cause involved is a virtuous act, then the consequence it produces can only be pleasure, and never pain. If the cause involved is a non-virtuous act, then the consequence it produces can only be pain, and never pleasure. Thus the first principle is that *actions are certain to produce similar consequences.*

2) The causes involved may be virtuous or non-virtuous acts which are relatively minor, but the consequences they each produce—the pleasure or the pain—will be of tremendous power. The second principle then is that *the consequences are greater than the actions.*

3) If one never performs the virtuous or non-virtuous action to act as a cause, he will never experience a consequence of either pleasure or pain. Thus the third principle: *One cannot meet a consequence if he has not committed an action.*

4) The fourth principle states that once a person has collected a virtuous or non-virtuous action to act as a cause, *once an action is committed, the consequence cannot be lost*—so long as the power of a good deed, for example, is not destroyed by an emotion like anger, or a bad deed by applying an appropriate antidote.[113]

There are other principles as well; it is said that whether the action is virtuous or non-virtuous, its power is multiplied if one performs it towards some especially important object. The same thing happens if the thought behind the action is particularly strong, or if the material with which one performs the deed is somehow special, or even if the person performing the deed is someone special.

You must try to gain some well-founded belief in these principles. Take time to contemplate even the most deep and subtle workings of actions and their consequences, and then put this understanding into actual practice. Putting the laws of action and consequence into practice means keeping them—and this means keeping the rules by avoiding the ten non-virtues.[114]

You've heard of the correct view that we call the "worldly" one—well this understanding of actions and consequences is what it refers to. This view by the way is something that everyone should adhere to, regardless of whether they're a monk or nun or layman. You should realize that the word "worldly" in this case is not just meant to refer to people who are still living the secular life. There is an expression we use, "ordinary people," to refer to any person who has yet to reach the path of a realized being.[115] Whatever else we may be, we are "worldly" people so long as we are ordinary people in this sense.

Putting religion into practice then must start from keeping the laws of actions and their consequences. It's been said that,

> The path begins with proper reliance on
>   a spiritual guide.
> The steps of the path begin with contemplating
>   your leisure and fortune.
> Meditation begins with your motivation; and
> Putting religion into practice begins with
>   observing the laws, of actions and
>   their consequences.[116]

Therefore we must never allow our body or speech or mind—any of the three doors through which we express ourselves—to be tainted by misdeeds. And if by some chance we do, we must purify ourselves of the misdeed through the process of confession.

Generally speaking, contemplation upon the principles of actions and their consequences is enough to stop desire for the future life. But really the main way is to contemplate the many sufferings of this cyclic life. In a broad sense, we can say that renunciation has just begun to sprout in a person's heart once he has meditated on the torments of "Revive" (the lightest hell) and feels a sense of terror.[117] But complete proficiency in renunciation comes only when one feels a total disgust even for the supposed good things of this revolving life.

The traditional contemplation of the sufferings of cyclic life has two parts: considering these sufferings in general, and thinking them over one by one. The text called *Word of the Gentle One* describes the individual sufferings first, and then goes on to the general ones.[118] The works known as *Path of Bliss* and *Quick Path,* on the other hand, present the general sufferings first and the individual sufferings later.[119] Each way of doing it conveys a very valuable lesson; here we will follow the *Word*.

Doing your best to follow the teaching on going for refuge, and to make the right decisions with regard to actions and their consequences, will free you from having to take one of the three lower births. But what you really need is to free yourself from the cycle of life altogether; for while you may have avoided a lower birth, achieving some wonderful life in one of the happier births is nothing but suffering anyway.

Let's say you are born as a human; still you must suffer as you come from the womb. Still you must suffer as your body gets older, day by day. Still you must suffer when you are ill. Still you must suffer as you die. You must suffer the pain of missing your beloved family. You must suffer the pain of encountering your hated enemies. You must suffer the pain of working for the things you want, and not being able to get them—and on and on.

Suppose you take the second type of happier birth—in some kind of heavenly place, as one of the lesser beings of pleasure. Still in your life you suffer during the fighting,[120] and suffer from intense jealousy towards the higher pleasure-beings, and suffer as your body is sliced apart or ripped to pieces, and on and on.

Suppose finally that you become one of the higher pleasure-beings. They live in all three realms of existence; let's say you get to be a being of pleasure in the first of them—in the realm of desire. Still you go through terrible suffering as after an incredibly long and pleasure-filled life the signs of death begin to ruin your body, and then as you take your fall to a lower birth, and on and on—for the vast majority of pleasure-beings go straight to one of the lives of misery. All the stored-up positive power of the good deeds they did in their past lives is squandered as they enjoy its consequences—the delights of a pleasure-being's existence. During this existence they have no chance to store up any more of this positive power. Still though they possess great supplies of bad deeds—tremendous negative power in the form of mental afflictions like desire and attachment. These then hurl them into a rebirth of misery when they die.

Or let's say lastly you can reach a birth as a being of pleasure in one of the higher two of the three realms of existence. These beings have no overt pain at all, but still by the very nature of life possess the most subtle form of suffering: the ever-present suffering of instant-by-instant aging. And these beings are totally helpless to keep themselves in their paradise; there always comes a day when the power of their past good deeds, which threw them there in the first place, finally runs dry. Then they touch the energy of one of their past bad deeds, and are forced to a lower birth. So you see, it doesn't really matter what wonderful things might come to you in the circle of life—none of them is stable, none of them is worth your trust. The very highest form of existence, that rare meditation level we call the "peak of life," is not the least bit better than the very lowest we can reach—hanging over a pot of molten steel in hell, about to be dipped in.

Lord Tsongkapa, in his great exposition on the Steps of the path to Buddhahood, divides the contemplation of life's general sufferings into three sections. These are contemplating the eight sufferings, the six sufferings, and the three sufferings. The group of eight though applies more to life as a human, and the group of three is given as sort of a summary. Here then we'll speak some of how to do the contemplation on the six sufferings.[121]

These six are as follows:

1) The problem that life has no certainty.
2) The problem that we always want more
   than we have.
3) The problem that we have to keep shucking
   off bodies, over and over again.
4) The problem that we have to keep going
   into a new life, over and over again.
5) The problem that we go up and down in our
   fortunes in life, over and over again.
6) The problem that no one can come along
   with us; ultimately we are alone.

These six problems are described at length in the standard works on the Steps to Buddhahood. We should remember though King Mefeed, whose last words were "There is no greater evil in the world than the fact that we always want more than we have."[122] You and I are monks, and there are only two things we should be doing:

> Read the holy books, get teaching on them,
>   contemplate their meaning.
> Live a life of rejection, and stay in
>   meditation.

Here a "life of rejection" means a life where we keep our morality, and reject bad deeds. If we can keep from going beyond these two activities, then one day we can become both wise and realized. If though we neglect these two, we will lose ourselves to what they call "lots of things to think about and lots of things to do." And then we won't do any spiritual practice at all. People make this mistake, by the way, because they are unable to stick to the precept of "Keep your wants few; be easy to satisfy."[123]

Since the three types of suffering are mentioned later on in our root text, we'll describe them briefly. All impure feelings of pain constitute the first type of suffering: the "suffering of suffering."

All impure feelings of pleasure constitute the second type of suffering: the "suffering of change." We can explain this suffering as follows. When you're in a place that's very hot, then something cool seems like pleasure. When you're in a place that's very cold, then something warm seems like pleasure. The same is true when you've had to walk a long way (sitting would seem a pleasure), or had to sit for a long time (walking would seem a pleasure).

None of these things that seem to be pleasure though is pleasure by nature, or pleasure in its very essence. If they were, then you would feel more pleasant the more you had of them. But this is not the case, for as you get more and more of them they too start to give you pain. When this happens we can understand that they are not pleasure by nature. They are, in fact, suffering—they are what we call the "suffering of change."

The third type of suffering is known as the "pervasive suffering, which brings in more." The point here is that, regardless which one of the six kinds of birth we take, we take on a body which, by its very existence, comes complete with its own particular sufferings built in. From the first moment we take the various impure parts of our being on, from the first moment of their existence, they provide a basis for all the sufferings we have to look forward to in life: birth, aging, sickness, death, and all the rest. The impure parts of ourselves are like a big pot, sucking in the suffering of suffering, sucking in the suffering of change, in both this and our future lives. We must find a way to stop taking births, to stop taking on all the impure parts we're made of. Until we do, our existence will be like lying on a bed of upright needles— never a thing but pain.

When we talk about "escaping cyclic life," it's not like running away from one country and managing to reach another. "Cyclic life" is precisely the continued existence of, the very fact of, the impure parts that make us up, the impure parts of our being that we've taken on. And when the continued existence of these parts is stopped at its root by the wisdom that realizes that nothing has a self-nature, this then is our "escape from cyclic life."

This completes our explanation of how to stop desire for your future lives.

X. HOW TO KNOW WHEN YOU'VE FOUND RENUNCIATION

The third and final section of our explanation of renunciation describes the point at which we can say a person has succeeded in developing it; as the next verse of the root text reads,

(5)

When you've meditated thus and feel not even
A moment's wish for the goods things of cyclic life,
And when you begin to think both night and day
Of achieving freedom, you've found renunciation.

Suppose *you've contemplated thus,* on the points already mentioned: your impermanence, the births of misery, the principles of actions and their consequences, and the sufferings of the happier births. And because of this you see for yourself that it's all meaningless: that even if you could achieve the kind of happiness that pleasure-beings enjoy in their paradises, it's really nothing but suffering; that until you can escape forever from cyclic life, this is the only way it will be.

And then it comes even stronger: in your heart, you *feel not even a moment's wish* even *for the* fantastic *riches* of the god-like beings they call Pure-one and Hundred-Gift; you feel no wish even for the wealth of a Wheel Emperor, who rules the world. And then a certain thought comes to your mind both *"night and day";* that is, in every conscious minute, the thought rushes into your mind on its own—the way a man with some great worry on his mind remembers his problem all in a rush, every time he wakes up during the night. *When you begin to think* this way *of achieving freedom,* when you genuinely want freedom this way, well then you know *you've found renunciation.*

Now the standard texts on the Steps to Buddhahood have sections ranging from the teaching on the difficulty of finding leisure and fortune, on up to instructions on renunciation, all included under the two headings of "paths for practicioners of lesser scope" and "paths for practicioners of medium scope."

Here in the *Three Principal Paths* though, they all come under the one heading of "renunciation." This is a unique feature of this work, and there is a reason for it. Renunciation is the one special cause that brings you what we call "great compassion"; to get this compassion, you must first find true thoughts of renunciation. Great compassion is a state of mind where you can absolutely no longer bear to see other beings tormented by the sufferings of life; there's no way you can achieve it as long as your concern about the way life torments you yourself is so feeble that it couldn't blow down a single upright hair. As the famous verses of *The Bodhisattva's Life* say,

> If people like these have never before
> Even in the dreams they dream
> Felt such a wish just for themselves,
> Then how can it come to them for others?[124]

Thus we can say that renunciation and compassion are the same state of mind, just that one is developed by meditating on your own situation, and the other by meditating on others' situation.

To develop this compassion, we must undertake to study and contemplate the Steps on the path to Buddhahood, that great teaching of the gentle protector Tsongkapa, and thus gradually train our minds. People like you and I see our feelings of desire, and our other mental afflictions, grow stronger day by day; the problem is that we have not even been able to train our minds in the paths for people of lesser and medium scopes of practice.

Intelligent people then should stop giving any thought to practicing mistaken paths that any local shaman or follower of some deficient "religion" could master: things like trying to develop extra-sensory powers, or the ability to perform miraculous feats, or the so-called "opening day" — pay-as-you-go religion. Discriminating people should instead learn, and contemplate, and meditate upon the three collections of scripture (which contain the important bulk of the teaching in general), and upon these Steps to Buddhahood (for they are the collected essence of the path of the three trainings).[125]

If you start off on these Steps, then you will never err, and will gradually gain the high meditative state called "quietude," and the three principal paths, and everything else on up to the two levels of the secret way. Any hope we have of attaining Buddhahood then rests upon this very teaching. And we must absolutely try to develop great compassion in our hearts; if we cannot develop this compassion, our Lama concluded, then there is no way at all we can develop the sublime wish to achieve Buddhahood, for the sake of every living being.

THE SECOND PATH:

THE WISH TO ACHIEVE ENLIGHTENMENT FOR EVERY LIVING BEING

XI. WHY YOU NEED THE WISH
FOR ENLIGHTENMENT

WE HAVE NOW reached the second of the four parts in the actual body of the text. This is an explanation of the wish to achieve enlightenment for the sake of every living being. This explanation itself will include three sections: why you need the wish for enlightenment, how to go about developing this wish, and how to know when you've finally developed it. The next verse of the root text tells us why we need this great wish:

(6)

Renunciation though can never bring
The total bliss of matchless Buddhahood
Unless it's bound by the purest wish; and so,
The wise seek the high wish for enlightenment.

You may be able to gain some fierce feelings of renunciation as we described it above; any good deeds you do under their influence though can only bring you an ordinary nirvana—they alone can never serve to bring you to omniscient enlightenment. We can see this from the fact that even practicioners of lower paths—people we call "listeners" and "self-made victors"—can possess true renunciation.[126]

For full enlightenment then a person needs to develop within his mind all three of the principal paths—and more specifically, he must have gained the second path: the wish to achieve enlightenment for every living being. You may possess extra-sensory powers, you may be able to perform miracles, you may have any number of fantastic qualities—but unless you have this precious jewel in your heart, you will never enter that select group of people who practice the greater way. Without this highest wish, none of your qualities will ever bring you total bliss — none of them; none of them at all, will bring you Buddhahood: the ability to free each and every living being from all the troubles of cyclic life, and from those of a lower escape from cyclic life.[127]

Those great practitioners of the lower paths — "enemy destroyers" of the "listener" or "self-made" type — possess fine qualities like a huge mountain made of pure gold; even such qualities as the ability to perceive emptiness directly. But these paths never bring them to Buddhahood. Why? Because they lack the wish to achieve enlightenment for every living being.[128]

If you do gain this great wish, you become a person who truly deserves to have the entire world — with all its different kinds of beings up to humans and gods — bow down at your feet, just as holy books like *The Bodhisattva's Life,* and *Entering the Middle Way,* and *The Rare Stack* describe it.[129] You find yourself in a different class of being, and then you completely outshine listeners and self-made victors — practitioners of the lower paths. Every virtuous act you do, even down to throwing a scrap of food to some wild bird, becomes a practice of the greater way; becomes a cause for your future Buddhahood; becomes the way of life of a bodhisattva.

If a person possesses this holy wish to achieve enlightenment for the sake of every living being, then all the countless Buddhas in all the ten directions of space look upon him as their son. And all the great bodhisattvas look upon him as their brother.

But that's not all; the whole question of whether you have reached the greater way, and the whole question of whether you will be able to achieve Buddhahood in this one short life, depend on whether you have truly gained this wish. So if you want enlightenment, our Lama concluded, you must train your thoughts in the wish.

XII. HOW TO DEVELOP THE WISH
FOR ENLIGHTENMENT

The second section in our explanation of the wish to achieve enlightenment for every living being describes how to develop this wish. As the next two verses say,

(7,8)

They're swept along on four fierce river currents,
Chained up tight in past deeds, hard to undo,
Stuffed in a steel cage of grasping "self,"
Smothered in the pitch-black ignorance.

In a limitless round they're born, and in
    their births
Are tortured by three sufferings without a break;
Think how your mothers feel, think of what's
    happening
To them: try to develop this highest wish.

We may begin with another pair of verses, from *The Bodhisattva's Life:*

Even just wishing you could stop
A headache another person has
Can bring you merit without measure
Because of the helpful intent you feel.

What need then to mention the wish
That you could stop the immeasurable pain
Of every being, and put every one
In a state of measureless happiness?[130]

The *Sutra that Viradatta Requested* says as well,

Were the merit of the wish for enlightenment
To take on some kind of physical form

95

It would fill the reaches of space itself
And then spill over farther still. [131]

The benefits of this wish to achieve enlightenment for all living beings are thus described, in these and other texts, as limitless. And so here are the mass of living beings, all of them our mothers, *swept along* the flow of *four river currents,* all *fierce suffering.* From one viewpoint, while they are acting as causes, these four are the torrent of desire, the torrent of views, the torrent of the ripe force of deeds, and the torrent of ignorance. Later, when they serve as results, they are the four torrents of birth, and aging, and illness, and death.

And these mother beings are not just hurtling along in these four great rivers; it's just as if their hands and feet too were bound fast—they are *chained up tight,* they are snared, *in* their own *past deeds, hard to undo.*

But that's not all; the bonds which hold them tight are no regular ties, like our twined ropes of yak-skin or hair. It's more like our mothers are clasped in fetters of iron, ever so hard to sever, ever so hard to unshackle—for while they are swept along they are *stuffed in a steel cage of grasping* to some non-existent *"self."*

And there's more. If there were some daylight, these mother beings would have some glimmer of hope—they could at least cry out, and try to get some help. But it is night, and the darkest hour of the night, and in pitch-black dark they are swept downstream the mighty river: they are *smothered* completely *in pitch-black ignorance.*

In a limitless round, in an endless round, *they are born* into the ocean of life, *and in these births they are tortured by three* different kinds of *suffering:* the suffering of suffering, the suffering of change, and the all-pervading suffering. And their torture comes to them *without a break*—it is always there.

This is *what's happening to them,* to our mother

beings, this is their situation: unbearable pain. There's nothing they can do like this to help themselves; the son though has a chance at hand to pull his mother free. He must find a way, and find it now, to grasp her hand and draw her out. And the way he must *try* is *to develop this* jewel *wish* for enlightenment: he must do so first by *thinking how* his *mothers feel,* tortured by pain; then by deciding to take personal responsibility, the duty of freeing them, upon himself; and so on, all in the proper stages.

To actually gain the wish for enlightenment he must first contemplate it. To contemplate it, he must first learn about it from another. "Loving-kindness" is an almost obsessive desire that each and every living being find happiness. "Compassion" is an almost obsessive desire that they be free of any pain. Think of how a mother feels when her one and only and most beloved son is in the throes of a serious illness. Wherever she goes, whatever she does, she is always thinking how wonderful it would be if she could find some way of freeing him quickly from his sickness. These thoughts come to her mind in a steady stream, without a break, and all of their own, automatically. They become an obsession with her. When we feel this way towards every living being, and only then, we can say we have gained what they call "great compassion."

Here in the teachings of the Buddha there are two methods given for training one's mind in this precious jewel, the wish for enlightenment. The first is known as the "seven-part, cause-and-effect instruction." The second we call "exchanging self and others." No matter which of the two you use to train your mind, you can definitely gain the wish for enlightenment. The way to train oneself in the wish, the way which is complete and which never errs, the way unmatched by any other here upon this earth, is the instruction of the Steps of the path to Buddhahood, the very essence of all the teachings of our gentle protector, the great Tsongkapa. Thus you should train your mind in the wish for enlightenment by using this very instruction.

Here we'll give just a brief summary of how one trains himself in the wish to achieve enlightenment for every living being. The start-off is to practice feelings of neutrality towards all beings; after that, one begins meditation on each of the steps from "mother recognition" on up. The first three steps are to recognize all beings as one's mothers, to feel gratitude for their kindness, and to wish to repay that kindness. These three act as a cause for what we call "beautiful" loving-kindness. This type of loving-kindness is itself the fourth step; it is both an effect brought about by the first three, and a cause for the fifth: great compassion.

The relative intensity of one's wish for enlightenment depends on the intensity of one's feeling of great compassion. If you find it difficult to develop compassion, you can practice the meditation known as "Lama Loving-Gaze" to help you gain it. If you make good efforts to perform this meditation and the proper supplications, as well as the practice where you visualize that your mind and that of Loving-Gaze are mixed inseparably, then you can gain a blessing for it.[132] This is a very special personal instruction for developing great compassion. There were, our Lama explained, a number of other profound points in this regard — but he would not detail them in a public gathering.

Once you develop great compassion, then you can develop the extraordinary form of personal responsibility, where you take upon yourself the load of working for others' benefit. And the wish to achieve enlightenment for every living being comes from this.

The meditation on neutrality goes like this. First you put your thoughts in an even state, free of feelings of like and dislike, by thinking about someone who is for you a neutral figure: neither your enemy nor your friend. Then you imagine that two people are sitting before you: one of your best-loved friends, and one of your ugliest enemies. Next you think very carefully about how the friend has, in many of your previous lives, taken birth as your enemy and hurt you. You think too about how the enemy has, in so many of your past lives, taken birth as your friend and helped you. This puts your mind in the even state, free of feelings of like and dislike.

You go on then to think about how all living beings are equal in that, from his own point of view, each one of them wants to be happy. They are equal too in not wanting pain. And they are equal in that every one has acted as both my enemy and my friend, many many times. So who am I supposed to like? And who am I supposed to dislike? You have to keep on practicing this way until, one day, you gain neutral feelings towards all sentient beings, as vast in extent as space itself.

The next step is the meditation where you recognize that every living being is your mother. Gaining this recognition is much easier if you apply the line of reasoning mentioned in the *Commentary on Valid Perception* for demonstrating the infinite regression of one's awareness. We'll present this reasoning here, in brief. [133]

Your awareness of today is a mental continuation of the awareness you had yesterday. This year's awareness is a mental continuation of the awareness you had the year before. Just so, your awareness over this entire life is a mental continuation of the awareness you had in your former life. The awareness you had in your former life was, in turn, a mental continuation of the awareness you had in the life before that. You can continue back in a regression like this and absolutely never reach some point where you can say, "Prior to this, I had no awareness." This then proves the infinite regression of one's awareness.

My own circle of life then must also be beginningless, and the births I have taken as well can have no starting point. There exists no place where I have never taken birth. I have taken birth in every single place, countless times. There exists no creature whose body I have not worn. I have worn every kind of body, countless times. Just the lives I have taken as a dog are themselves beyond any number to count. And the same is true for every living being.

Therefore there exists no being who has never been my mother. Absolutely every single one of them has been my mother a countless number of times. Even the number of times that each has been my mother in just my births as a human is past all counting too.

Do this meditation over and over until you gain a deep-felt certainty that each and every living being has been your mother, over and over, countless times.

Developing a sense of gratitude is the next step, and you can start by taking your mother in this present life. She began her hardships for me while I was still in her womb, gladly taking it upon herself to avoid anything she felt might hurt me — even down to the food she ate — treating herself with care, as though she were sick. For nine months and ten days she carried me in her womb, looking at her own body as though it belonged to someone else, someone very ill, and hesitating even to take big steps.

As she gave me birth, my mother was torn with violent suffering, excruciating pain, and yet still felt an overwhelming joy, as though she had discovered some precious gem that would grant her any wish.

Right then I knew absolutely nothing more than to cry and wave my arms around somehow. I was totally helpless. Totally stupid. Incapacitated. Nothing more than some baby chick with a red-rubber beak still yet to harden. But she swayed me on her fingertips, and pressed me to her body's warmth, and greeted me with a smile of love.

With joyful eyes she gazed on me, and wiped the snot

from my face with her lips, and cleaned my filthy shit with her hands. Sometimes she chewed my food for me, and fed me things like milky porridge straight from her mouth to mine. She did her best to protect me from any hurt. She did her best to get me any good.

In those days I had to look to her for everything; good or bad, happy or sad, all the hope I could have lay in one person: mother. But for her kindness, I wouldn't have lasted an hour; they could have set me out in the open right then and some birds or a dog would have come and made a meal of me—I'd have no hope of coming out alive. Every single day she protected me from harms that could have taken my life, no less than a hundred times. Such was her kindness.

And while I was growing up she gathered together whatever I needed, avoiding no bad deed, and no suffering, and caring nothing for what other people might say of her. All the money and things she had she handed over to me, hesitating to use anything for herself.

For those of us who are fortunate enough to be practicing the monastic life, it was Mother who put forth all the necessary expenses, giving without reservation, to arrange our admission into the monastery. And from that time on she supported us here, from whatever resources she had. Thus the kindness she has shown us is truly without measure.

And this is not the only life in which my present mother has given this kindness to me. She has showered me with this kindness, great kindness, over and over, countless times, in my many lives before. And she is not the only one; every single living being has been my mother in my past lives, and during those lives cared for me no less than my present mother does—it is only my transitions from death to birth that prevent me from recognizing all these mothers now.

Look now, concluded our Lama, at the way any common animal—a dog or bird, even the tiny sparrow—

shows affection for its young, and cares for it well. From watching this we can imagine what kindness we were given too.

The next step in gaining the wish for enlightenment is to develop a wish to repay this great kindness. So every living being is my mother, and has given me her loving care over and over endlessly, for time with no beginning. And we know from what was described above that they are being swept along by four great currents, out to sea — to the vast expanse of the ocean of cyclic life. They are tormented, without a break, by the three types of suffering, and all the other pains. Their situation is desperate.

And here am I, their child. Right now I have a chance to rescue them from this ocean of cyclic life. Suppose I simply sit and bide my time, and give no thought to them. This is the lowest a person could stoop — base and absolutely shameless.

Right now I could give them things that they would be happy to get — food, or clothes, or beds to sleep on, whatever. But these are only some temporary happiness within the circle of life. The very highest way of repaying their kindness would be to put them into the state of ultimate happiness. So let me decide within myself that every living being must come to have every happiness. And every one should be freed as well from every form of pain.

Right now it's absurd to say that these beings have any kind of pure happiness — they don't even have any of the impure kinds. Every single thing they think is happiness is, in its essence, nothing more than pain. They want wantables but don't want to know about doing the good deeds that bring happiness. They want no unwantables but don't want to know about giving up the bad deeds that bring pain. They act ass backwards: they do what they shouldn't and don't what they should. And so my dear aged mothers, these living beings, are made to suffer.

"How good it would be if they could all find
every happiness, and every cause of happiness.
I wish they could. I'll see that they do."

"How good it would be if they could all be free
of every pain, and every cause of pain. I wish
they could. I'll see that they do."

Let these two trains of thought run through your
mind; meditate on them over and over again. Then you
will come to feel the very strongest loving-kindness and
compassion.

Some people might come up with the idea that "Why
should I take upon myself this great load, of every living
being? There are plenty of Buddhas and bodhisattvas
around to guide them on their way." This kind of
thought though is absolutely improper. It's base. It's
shameless. It's as if your mother in this life was hungry,
and parched, and you expected someone else's child to go
and give her food and drink. But it's you for whom she
has cared, and the responsibility of paying her back has
fallen only to you.

It's the same with all these living beings, who for
beginningless time have served as my mother so many
times, and who in each of these times cared for me in
every way with the kindness of this present mother.
Returning their kindness is no business of anyone else at
all, not for some Buddha or bodhisattva—it is my
responsibility, and only mine.

So someone is going to do it—to make sure every sentient being has every happiness, and never a single pain. It
is going to be myself; I'll rely on no one else. I by myself
will see to it that every single being comes to have every
single happiness. And I by myself will see to it that every
single being gets free of every single pain. I will by myself
put them into the state of the Lama, the state of Buddhahood. Meditate strongly on these thoughts; they are the

step we call the "extraordinary form of personal responsibility."

I may be able to develop this noble intention, but the fact is that I'm completely incapable of leading a single being to Buddhahood—much less every one of them. Who then has the capacity? This power is had by a fully enlightened Buddha—only by him, and by no one else at all. If I can reach the same state, I will by definition have brought both mine and others' benefit to its perfection. And then every single ray of light that emanates from me, whether it be an action of my body, or my speech, or my thoughts, will have the power to accomplish the ends of countless sentient beings.

And so, for the sake of every living being, I will do anything I can to achieve this one great goal—the state of a Buddha—with every speed. Think this way to yourself, and do anything you can to develop the genuine wish to reach enlightenment for every living being.

While you practice these meditations to develop the wish for enlightenment, you can also reflect that—when you achieve Buddhahood—you will by the way automatically gain everything you need for yourself as well. Our Lama mentioned that this point was stated in Lord Tsongkapa's exposition on the Steps of the path as being very helpful in preventing a person from slipping to the lesser way.[134]

The first three of the seven parts in this cause-and-effect instruction provide a foundation for great compassion. The "beautiful" form of loving-kindness comes out as a result of these three, so there is no separate meditation instruction for it.[135] One must though in its place meditate upon the loving-kindness where you wish that every being gain every happiness.

This loving-kindness, as well as compassion and the extraordinary type of personal responsibility, are all forms of an attitude of striving for the welfare of others. The actual wish for enlightenment is their result. The works on the Steps of the path themselves have a similar structure. The paths for people of lesser and medium scopes represent a preliminary to developing the wish for enlightenment. The teaching on how to meditate on this great wish is the main stage. In conclusion then come the sections on bodhisattva deeds—advices in acting out the wish.

When you're practicing to develop this wish for enlightenment, you should train your mind in its basic nature and all its various attributes: these include the twenty-two forms of the wish, the distinction between praying and actually engaging, and so on.[136]

This precious jewel, the wish to gain enlightenment for every being, is the inner essence of all the high teachings of the victorious Buddhas. It is the single centermost contemplation of every one of their sons—the bodhisattvas. As *The Bodhisattva's Life* relates,

> It's the purest essence of the butter
> Churned from the milk of the holy word.

We see too,

> Many eons the Able Lords considered,
> And found but this to be of benefit.[137]

Our gentle protector, the great Tsongkapa, has as well composed the lines that begin with "Center beam of the highest way, the wish . . ." and conclude with " . . . Bodhisattva princes, knowing this, / Keep the high jewel wish their center practice."[138] It was only this precious wish for enlightenment, and nothing else at all, that the all-knowing Lord ever described as the "center practice." Therefore those of us who wish to become followers of the greater way must make the wish for enlightenment our very centermost practice.

Nowadays when you go up to someone and ask him what his very most important practice is, he'll tell you he's meditating on one of those powerful tutelary deities. You don't meet people who say their chief practice is meditating on the wish to achieve enlightenment for every living being. Much less, for in fact it's quite difficult to find anyone who even realizes that he should make this wish his centermost practice.

We see people making all different sorts of things their central practice: the Elimination Ritual for getting rid of bad spirits, the Golden Tea offering, the Spell for Ending Evil Litigation, the ritual they call Stopping All Harms, the Sheep Spell, the Horse Spell, the Money Spell, the ritual for No More Problems, the ritual for Stopping Bad Luck at the End of the Twelve-Year Cycle, the ritual for Preventing the Praise that Others Give You from Turning to a Curse, and on and on. These are all so bad that they make it look pretty good when a person can say he's making a central practice out of anything at all associated with some authentic tutelary deity.[139]

We also see a number of works gaining some popularity in different localities that seem to be just anything somebody could think up: the String of Jewels for those Bound by Blood, the Blade of Gold for Confessing Sins, the so-called "Dog Sutra," the so-called "Wolf Sutra," the so-called "Fox Sutra," the so-called "Bear Sutra," the so-called "Snake Sutra," and all the rest. We find though absolutely no legitimate origin for any of these works.

If you really do need a text to use for confessing your bad deeds, you should stop wasting your time with fake scriptures and meaningless efforts like these. The Victors have, in all their open and secret teachings, given us more than enough appropriate works: the *Three Heaps Sutra,* the *Sublime Medicine Sutra,* the *Sutra of the Great Freedom,* the *Sutra of the Eon of Fortune,* and others of the like.[140] It is texts like these, our Lama told us, authoritative texts with a legitimate origin, that we must use for our study and recitations.

Now there are also some people around who think to themselves, "But I *do* have the wish for enlightenment. After all, at the beginning of all my devotions I recite the 'Buddha-Dharma-Sangha' prayer[141] and think about achieving Buddhahood so I could help every living being." This though is just expressing a hope that you gain the wish for enlightenment—it's just making a prayer about the wish. It's not the actual wish itself. If it were, then developing the wish to achieve Buddhahood would have to be the very easiest of all the many practices of virtue we are supposedly trying to do. And so, concluded our Lama, we must rather gain this true wish by putting our minds through the training described above—one by one through each of the steps, in order.

XIII. HOW TO KNOW WHEN YOU'VE FOUND THE WISH FOR ENLIGHTENMENT

This brings us to the third and final section in our explanation of the wish for enlightenment: how to know when you've finally developed it. This point is covered with great detail in various works, including both the more extensive and the briefer presentations on the Steps of the path to enlightenment, which at this point employ material from the first of the *Stages of Meditation*.[142] To put it briefly, suppose a mother has watched her beloved child slip down into a pit of red-hot coals. The fire is searing his body. She cannot stand to see it go on for a single second. She throws herself forward to pull the child out.

All the living creatures of the universe, all our dear mothers, are burning in the same way, in the unbearable pain of the three lower realms, and the circle of life in general. When we cannot stand to see it go on for a single second more, when we finally feel the true wish to reach total enlightenment, immediately, for the sake of every living being, well then—our Lama concluded—you can say you have gained the wish for enlightenment.

THE THIRD PATH:
CORRECT VIEW

XIV. WHY YOU NEED CORRECT VIEW

WE HAVE NOW reached the third of the four parts of the body of the text: the explanation of correct view. Here there are five sections; the first, which explains why you need to meditate on correct view, is expressed in the next verse of the root text:

(9)

You may master renunciation and the wish,
But unless you have the wisdom perceiving reality
You cannot cut the root of cyclic life.
Make efforts in ways then to perceive interdependence.

What the verse is saying is this: "Unless you have that very profound correct view about suchness—unless you have the wisdom that perceives reality, or ultimate truth—you can strive to perfect renunciation and the wish for enlightenment (along with all the other 'method' practices) as much as you please; but you cannot cut the root of cyclic life, grasping to a 'self,' since these practices alone do not act as a direct antidote for your grasping."

And that's not all. A person without this profound view may be able to attain various levels on up to the first of the five paths of the greater way, the "accumulation" path, by force of renunciation and the wish for enlightenment alone. But he can never go any further. And if he is a follower of the lesser way he cannot even reach the second of its paths, the path of "preparation."[143]

Suppose though that your mind is completely filled with thoughts of renunciation and the wish to achieve enlightenment for every living being, and then in addition you open your eyes to this profound view. Now you can achieve all the various levels and paths of the greater way, from its second path (also called "preparation") on up. Then too the things you do take on a very special power, to bring about for you the states of freedom and all-knowing.

All of us sitting here have decided that we will take it upon ourselves to liberate living beings. But unless we find some actual way of liberating them, this will never be more than some noble intent. Thus at the very start we have to gain an outlook that says, "I am going to go and find the final form of that profound view that cuts the root of cyclic life." Now there is a kind of correct view that we call the "worldly" type; with it, you perceive the laws of actions and their consequences. This view alone though is not enough. It too, by the way, is ultimately tied to the view with which you realize that no self exists.

Certain non-Buddhist sages can put themselves into a deep, single-pointed state of meditation—and they attain all eight levels of concentration and formlessness.[144] But they lack the view with which you realize no self exists, and fail therefore even to reduce their harmful emotions slightly—much less to eliminate them. As the sutra called *King of Concentration* says,

> The worldly meditate on concentration
> But it doesn't destroy their concept of a self.
> This feeds their unhealthy thoughts, stirs them up,
> And ends like the meditation of Udraka.[145]

Our tendency to grasp to some "self" is the very root of our circling life. To cut this root we absolutely must gain the view that perceives that no such self exists. As the same work says,

112

Suppose you analyze, see the no-self of things,
And suppose you meditate on what you've seen;
It leads you to the result of gaining nirvana—
Nothing else can lead you to this peace.

To win freedom you must eliminate, from its root, this
grasping to a "self." To eliminate it, you must meditate
on how nothing has a self: you must find a path or
mental viewpoint which holds things in a way that is
completely incompatible with the way you now grasp for
a "self." You can make any great efforts you want in
practices like charity and morality, but without this meditation on no-self you will never be able to attain freedom. As the *400 Verses* says, "There is no second door to
peace."[146] This wisdom which perceives that no self exists
is then a "without which nothing" for freeing yourself
from the circle of life.

Wisdom though is not enough by itself either. Compassion too is a "without which nothing." And this is why
we say you must have both "method" and "wisdom,"
never one without the other. As we read in the *Sutra of
Vimalakirti,*

Wisdom not steeped in method is bondage.
Wisdom steeped in method is freedom.
Method not steeped in wisdom is bondage.
Method steeped in wisdom is freedom.[147]

The result we want to achieve is the two bodies of an
enlightened being: the "dharma body" and the "form
body." To get them, we must gather together a perfect
union of two great masses of goodness. To do this we
must rely on method and wisdom, one always with the
other. As our glorious savior, the realized being Nagarjuna, has written:

By this virtue may all beings
Gather the masses of merit and wisdom.
May they achieve the ultimate two
That the merit and the wisdom produce.[148]

The illustrious Chandrakirti has said as well,

On vast wide-spreading wings of both
  the conventional and the real
The king goose flies on at the center
  point in the formation
Of the other geese, all beings, spurred
  by the wind of virtue,
Reaching to the farthest shore of the ocean
  of Victors' qualities.[149]

Here the word "conventional" refers to "method"; that
is, the wish to achieve enlightenment for every sentient
being. "Reality" refers to "wisdom"—meaning correct
view. A great bird with both wings complete can soar
unimpeded in the sky; just so, a person who wants to
travel to that farthest shore where he possesses each and
every good quality of the victorious Buddhas must have
method and wisdom—the wish for enlightenment and
correct view—and he must have them both together. A
person who has one without the other is like a bird with a
broken wing. He cannot make the journey.

"How then do I gain this view?" you may ask. Not just
anything will do: you must rather follow one of the scriptures taught by the enlightened Conquerers—a true
teaching, and one which treats the "literal." Generally
speaking, we draw the distinction between "literal" and
"figurative" as follows: something is "literal" when its
nature actually lies in the ultimate, and something is
"figurative" when its nature does not lie in the ultimate.
"Literal" scriptures then are those that deal chiefly with

ultimate truth, while other types of scriptures we call "figurative."

Not every ancient sage was capable of clarifying the true meaning of the literal and figurative scriptures. For commenting on the true intent of the "literal" it took the savior Nagarjuna, as foretold by the Buddhas themselves. He was able to introduce an entire system clarifying the "literal" and profound view just as the victorious Buddhas intended it. He did so through the *Root Wisdom* and other works in his famed "Collection on the Reasoning of the Middle Way," basing them all on the scripture known as *Understanding that Has No End.*[150]

Later on came the masters Buddhapalita, author of the commentary that bears his name, and Aryadeva—who composed the *400 Verses on the Middle Way* and other titles. Most especially there was Master Chandrakirti who, following the intent of the realized being Nagarjuna, wrote various works including *A Clarification of the Words* (which explains the wording of Master Nagarjuna's *Root Wisdom*) and *Entering the Middle Way* (which enters into the meaning of the *Root*).[151]

Here in the Land of Snows, in Tibet, it was the gentle protector Tsongkapa—and no one else but him—who was able to elucidate the true meaning of these works with absolute accuracy, without the slightest taint of error. Thus you and I should follow the excellent system of that highest of realized beings, Nagarjuna, and his spiritual sons; we should rely on the great textbooks of the omniscient Lord Tsongkapa, on his high and wondrous words. As *Entering the Middle Way* states,

> There's no way to peace for people who've
> stepped from the path
> Of the system taught by the Master Nagarjuna.
> They've lost the truths, the conventional
> and the real;
> Those who've lost the truths cannot be free.[152]

The matchless Lord Atisha has said as well:

> Nagarjuna's student was Chandrakirti;
> The instructions handed down from them
> Bring you to see reality, truth.[153]

You can see then that this profound viewpoint on things is indispensable for both the open and the secret teachings.

Broadly speaking, there were four great schools of Buddhist thought that came out of India—the "land of the realized." Members of the Vatsiputriya section of the "Detailist" school[154] assert that what we seek to see does not exist is any self which is unchanging, and singular, and independent. Other members of the Detailist school, as well as those of the "Scripturalist" school,[155] teach that what we seek to deny is something that can stand on its own, something which exists in a substantial way.

The "Mind-Only" school[156] says that what we come to realize does not exist is any case where the subject that holds an object and the object which it holds are made from any different "substance."[157] What we call the "Independent," one part of the Middle Way school,[158] believes that what we come to refute is any object that exists in some unique way of its own, rather than being established as an existent thing simply by virtue of its having appeared to an unaffected awareness.[159]

The "Implication" section of the Middle Way school,[160] finally, teaches that what we come to see has no existence is an object which exists from its own side, rather than simply existing through a concept supplied from our side.

Here in the verses of the *Three Principal Paths* our gentle protector, the great Tsongkapa, has urged us to try to perceive interdependence; as the line goes, "Make efforts in ways then to perceive interdependence." This he does instead of telling us to "Make efforts in ways to perceive emptiness," and for an extremely important reason.

Different schools have different ways of explaining "interdependence." The "Functionalist" group[161] says that when something is "interdependent," it's because it has come about through various causes and conditions. This doesn't allow them to establish interdependence for those objects which are unchanging, and have no causes.

The "Independent" group has a way of describing interdependence that's a little bit better. They say that something is interdependent whenever it exists in dependence upon its parts. They then can establish interdependence with both changing and unchanging objects: for those with causes and without.

The way the last group, the one we call "Implication," decides that something is interdependent is subtler than all the rest. They say that something is interdependent when we have taken two things—a reasonable basis to be given a name and a reasonable idea to give it a name—and come out with an object we gave a name.

This subtle form of interdependence is not itself the way to perceive emptiness, but there is a good reason why we present interdependence—in the cause-and-effect interpretation accepted by all the schools—here at the very outset. First of all it prevents students from swinging to the opposite extreme where they believe that, if all things are empty, they can have no existence at all. Secondly, a correct understanding of interdependence does lead one to the way of perceiving emptiness. And so, concluded our Lama, there is crucial significance to presenting the instructions on interdependence first—as the first step on the way to perceiving emptiness.

XV. WHAT IS CORRECT VIEW?

The second of the five points in our discussion of the third principal path addresses the question: what is correct view? The answer appears in the next verse of the root text.

(10)

A person's entered the path that pleases the Buddhas
When for all objects, in the cycle or beyond,
He sees that cause and effect can never fail,
And when for him they lose all solid appearance.

The line here about "when for all objects" gives us the subject under consideration: what we will see is empty. The line with the words "cause and effect" is meant to give us the classic logical reason for proving things are empty: "because they are interdependent." The line with "they lose all solid appearance" presents us the premise that the reason is meant to prove.

The expression "all objects" refers to each and every object from basic physical matter on up to the omniscience of a Buddha. They all exist in dependence upon their parts, so in a manner of speaking their "cause and effect can never fail." The antithesis, which we seek to disprove, is that these objects could have the solid existence they appear to have: that they could exist naturally. "When they lose all solid appearance" — that is, when we perceive that there is not a single thing in the universe which has any true or natural existence — then we have found "the path that pleases the Buddhas."

If we look for the very root that keeps you and I going round in this circle of life, we come down to ignorance, to our grasping for a "self." To cut this root, we must develop wisdom which perceives that no such "self" exists. If we were to discuss what no-self is in any detailed way, it would be best to apply a number of sections from the works on the Steps to the path; one example would be the "fourfold analysis."[162] Here though we will give only a brief presentation of the most vital points concerning correct view, and we will use the classical reasoning based on interdependence.

Now every existent object is a product of something to be given a name and something else to give it a name. There is not a single atom of anything in the universe which does not rely on this process—there is nothing which exists from its own side. I too then am a product: someone has taken two things together, my body and my mind, and called it "me." I am nothing more than that. There is no "me" which exists from its own side; there is no "me" which does not rely on someone taking my body and mind together and granting it the name. Neither in fact do my body or my mind themselves exist from their own sides.

We can express all this in the classical form of a logical statement:

> Consider all objects, those of the cycle
> and those beyond it.
> They have none of the true and solid existence
> that I hold them to have; they cannot
> exist on their own,
> Because they are interdependent.

What we mean here by "interdependence" is that all objects are interrelated with others on which they depend; that is, they occur through dependence on other objects. This is why there is absolutely no way they can exist on their own.

We can take for example the way we appoint the chanting master of a monastery, or the governor of some district, or any similar figure. First there must be a reasonable basis to be called "chanting master": there must be a person who is worthy of being the chanting master.

Then there must be someone like the abbot of the monastery who says, "He is now the chanting master." Until the abbot does so, until the abbot applies the name and the concept to this person, he cannot be the chanting master—even though he may have all the qualities you need to be named "chanting master."

If this were not the case, and if the person were somehow the chanting master from the beginning, all on his own without anyone putting the name or idea on him, then he would have to have been the chanting master all along—from the time he lay in his mother's womb. And when he was born, the moment he came out of her womb, people then should have said, "Here comes the chanting master!"

But people didn't say it, because getting to be the chanting master depends on many other factors. We don't call someone "chanting master" until there is a basis to give the name—a monk who is fit to be chanting master, and until a person qualified to give him the name hangs it on him, and says "This is the chanting master." Neither until this time does the person himself think "I am the chanting master." But once the concept has been applied to him, "You are the chanting master," then people start to talk about him as "chanting master," and he too begins to think "I am the chanting master."

The case is the same with something like a horse. We take the body and the mind of the horse, and we put them together— we take all the proper causes and conditions together—and label them with the name "horse." A building is the same too: nothing but a name put on a certain collection of parts that act as the basis to receive the name.

And the same goes for every existing entity: they are nothing but a name and a concept, "This we call this, and that we call that," applied to the collection of parts that acts as the basis of the particular entity's name. There does not exist the single tiniest bit of anything that is some kind of object on its own, divorced of the parts we give its name.

"Well then," you might think to yourself, "if every object is nothing more that what we label it, then I can go out and call gold 'brass,' or call a pillar a 'pitcher,' and that's just what they will be." But it's not; we do say that things are just labelled what they are, but for the label to be applied, the basis that gets it must be a reasonable one for the particular label.

When we apply a label, three conditions must be present. The three are as follows: (1) the object must be known to a conventional perception; (2) no other conventional perception can contradict its existence; and (3) no ultimate analysis can contradict its existence either. All three must be there.

Now here is what we mean when we say that one conventional perception has been contradicted by another. We can be standing looking at a scarecrow way off in the distance, and someone next to us says "That's a man over there," and we believe him. Then someone comes up who's seen for himself that the thing is a scarecrow and tells us "It's just a scarecrow." Our initial perception of the thing as a man then vanishes. This is an indication that the basis was not a reasonable one for the given name.

That's not all—we can go around giving out all sorts of names, we can say "Rabbits have horns," but that's not going to make the horns exist; there's no reasonable basis to get the label. Therefore we must have a reasonable, conventional state of mind that is applying a name to a reasonable collection of parts which acts as the basis we want to give the name—and which actually exists.

Thus too when we go to name somebody governor of a district we have to have a person who is suitable to be given the name—we must have a reasonable basis for our label. We don't take some deaf-mute bastard kid and appoint him governor.

If any of these things existed from its own side, it wouldn't have to rely on the group of parts we give its name, and then each one would have to exist out there, on its own. But that's not the way it is: they can only exist in dependence on the group of parts we give their name. And this is why they do not exist from their own side, and they do not exist naturally, and they do not exist truly.

We can take some local chieftain; he is chief only so far as we on our part call him "chief," and not out there from his own side. To us though the chief appears to exist out there on his own, and we take him to be this way. A chief that could exist as we take him to is just what we want to see does not exist.

This "me" is the same way too. It is not something that exists out there on top of my body and mind. Rather, it is only something that appears to me only because I have applied the name: I have taken the collection of parts and put upon them the label and concept of "me": the "me" is only in name.

The process of labelling occurs like this. The basis to be given the name exists out there. From our side come the concept that applies the name and the name itself. We come out then with something labelled — and it's nothing more than that.

We can illustrate this with a building. Say that someone has just put up three new buildings, each with the same attractive design. They cannot be the "sleeping quarters" or anything else from the very beginning, before they are given their separate names. But then the owner comes and puts a different name on each building: he says, "This one will serve as the sleeping quarters, and this one will be the kitchen facility," and so on. Only after this do we think to ourselves, "These are the sleeping quarters," or "This is the kitchen facility" — and only then do each of them exist as such. We can have a basis to get the name — the group of buildings — but until the one to give them the name actually does so, they're not the three. Thus a building too is nothing more than something labelled with a name and a concept. And we are talking about more than just some building; the point is that any existent entity is just the same: we must take it to be a product of the labelling process, and not the basis which receives our label.

This applies equally to the conventional "me"—it only exists insofar as I label it with some concept. You and I tend to think of "me" as something more than just a creation of names; we have this vivid mental image of him out there on his own, the intimate experiencer of all that he feels, pleasure or pain or whatever. The state of mind that clutches to "me" this way is what we call "inborn grasping to a self," or the "inborn destructible view."[163] And the oh-so-vivid, self-standing "me" that this state of mind clings to is the self that we must come to see does not exist. As the glorious Chandrakirti has said as well,

Here what we call "self" refers to any nature or state objects could have in which they relied on nothing else. The non-existence of this is what we call "no-self."[164]

Now the conventional "me"—the one that does exist—is only something we've created with a label, using some basis to take the label and some idea to give the label. This is what those lines in the ritual for the secret Frightener teaching are referring to as they start off, "Since every object is labelled, in dependence . . ."[165] The same sentiment is expressed, among other places, in the ritual for the secret teaching of Highest Bliss: "Like an illusion, just labelled with a concept."[166]

If we really get into fine detail, we must analyze not the way that objects appear to us, but rather how we grasp them. Thus it is too with the object we want to see does not exist: it is not that we will deny what appears to us, but rather what we grasp. This then can be like our refrain:

> Let me realize that these things are labelled,
>   creations of concepts;
> That they can exist only in dependence on a basis
>   to receive a name and someone to give the
>   name;
> That they occur in dependence on many
>   other factors;
> That they don't exist out there, on their own.

Let's talk then about the thing we will see does not exist, in terms of the object we grasp. When we start to examine whether it exists or not, the image that comes to our mind is not the "me" that we have created with our labels, but rather some "me" that looks like it exists out there, on his own. The object we grasp therefore consists not of the "me" which is nothing but a label applied to our body and mind, but rather of the "me" which seems to exist out there on its own, on top the body and the mind together.

Let's say for example that dusk has fallen and you see some piece of rope with a checkered pattern. At first you put a name onto it and think to yourself, "Oh my! A snake!" After that you forget it was you who put the name on it and it starts to look like a snake out there on its own. The way that it looks just then is *not* what we want to see doesn't exist. Rather what we want to deny is *what we grasp:* that the thing we hold could really exist the way it looks to us to exist.

It's just the same when we investigate this idea of "me." Suppose someone comes up and calls you out by name. At first the "me" that appears to you is simply the conventional one: you think to yourself, "He's calling me." But then he says to you, "So you're the thief!" or something like that. Then your "me" starts getting stronger and stronger; you start thinking to yourself "Why is he pointing the finger at me? It wasn't me who stole it. They can't blame ME!" You start saying "me" "me" and the "me" starts looking like a "me" that can stand on its own, a very vivid "me."

Now we are not denying the existence of the ordinary, conventional "me" that first appeared to you. Nor are we denying that "me" appeared to stand on its own, that it appeared to truly exist. We are not even denying the "me" that appears to stand on its own, the "me" that appears to truly exist. Rather we are denying that "me" could actually stand on its own, that "me" could actually exist naturally: we are denying any "me" that could actually naturally exist.

And when you deny this "me," when you see that this "me" does not exist — when for your this so-vivid "me" that stands out there on his own without relying on the two of mind and body ceases to be, and all that's left is simple emptiness of him, then as the sages say you have first found the "view of the middle way." And then you have found the "path that pleases the Victors."

When you do this sort of analysis, and you seek the thing with the name, you will never be able to find a single atom of anything in the universe that exists in itself. All the normal workings of the world though are quite logical and proper; things make other things happen, things do what they do, though all in only an apparent way, in a conventionally agreed-upon way.

A building for example can be without a single atom of "true" existence, and yet so long as the causes and conditions for the building have come together — so long as it exists solely by virtue of a name and our concept of it — then it can do everything a building is supposed to do, and perfectly so. The reflection of some object in a mirror too may never be more than just something that appears to the mind and gets itself a name, it may never win any endorsement as being the object itself, but it can still exhibit all the normal workings of causation; the reflection may be nothing more than an apparition, but it can still show you whether you have a spot on your face, or whatever. This then is why we say that "to exist, it's enough to exist conventionally; but not existing ultimately, is not enough to not exist."

Any person who really understands interdependence in the sense that we've just described it begins to develop a strong recognition of the laws of actions and their consequences—they become more and more important for him.

And this is why. First of all, good deeds lead to pleasure and bad deeds lead to pain; each cause is connected to its own result—it can never go wrong somehow and produce the other result. This invariable relationship comes from interdependence.

Once you understand the sense in which "interdependence" refers to lack of any natural existence, then you understand by implication that interdependence in the form of cause and effect is, in a merely conventional way, entirely proper or infallible. This then allows you to gain a total conviction towards the laws that govern all actions and consequences—whether they be those within the circle of life or those that are beyond it.

We can say then that, because it depends on some other group of things, no object can exist naturally. And the fact that nothing exists naturally is what makes cause and effect perfectly plausible. And the fact that all the workings of cause and effect are perfectly plausible is what allows seeds to turn to sprouts, and sprouts to grains, and all the rest.

Suppose this were not the case, and seeds of barley or whatever existed naturally—then they could never turn into sprouts. Neither could children ever turn into adults, or anything of the like ever occur, if they all existed naturally. If the higher births existed naturally, then it would be impossible for a person in a higher birth to fall into the hells. If ordinary living beings existed naturally, then it would be impossible for such a being to become a Buddha, and so forth—the logical problems of being something "naturally" are many.

What we've said above, concluded our Lama, conveys a teaching which is therefore unique to the "Implication" section of the Middle Way school: that these two principles—cause and effect, or interdependence, and the fact that nothing exists naturally—go hand in hand, each supporting the other.

XVI. HOW TO KNOW WHEN YOUR ANALYSIS IS STILL INCOMPLETE

The third of the five sections in our treatment of correct view explains how to know when the analysis you are conducting with the view you have is still incomplete. This point is brought out in the next verse of the root text:

(11)

You've yet to realize the thought of the Able
As long as two ideas seem to you disparate:
The appearance of things—infallible interdependence;
And emptiness—beyond taking any position.

Let's say you've meditated on the instructions we've given above. You are directing your view to analyze all phenomena. If your analysis is really complete, then interdependence and emptiness must appear to you to go hand in hand, supporting each other.

Despite this fact, it appears that people like some of the ancient Indian sages, and the earlier Tibetan Buddhists as well, who made it seem like they had grasped the concept of no self-nature nonetheless did not understand how to explain interdependence.

What the verse is saying then, concluded our Lama, is this: "Suppose you do have some understanding of the two concepts individually: of (1) the *'appearance of things,'* or interdependence, *and* (2) *emptiness*—the fact that nothing exists naturally. But suppose to you they seem like contradictory characteristics—you think that no object could possess one, and still possess the other.

"Consider these *two ideas:* (1) *infallible interdependence,* where causes (that is, actions) of a certain kind must always lead to results (consequences) of the same kind; and (2) emptiness, the idea *beyond taking any position*--the fact that no existent object in the universe contains a single atom of something that can exist on its own.

"For such time as they appear this way to you—so long as *the two ideas seem to you* mutually exclusive, like hot and cold—then *you've yet to realize* perfectly the ultimate point of *the thought of the Able* Ones, the Buddhas."

XVII. HOW TO KNOW WHEN YOUR ANALYSIS IS COMPLETE

This brings us to the fourth section: how to know when the analysis you are performing with the view you've developed is complete. This is explained in the next verse of the root text:

(12)

At some point they no longer alternate,
     come together;
Just seeing that interdependence never fails
Brings realization that destroys how you
     hold to objects,
And then your analysis with view is complete.

Now here's what we mean when we say that "at some point they no longer alternate." We take two things: first, the fact that everything about the way things work, and about good deeds and bad deeds, is perfectly proper, despite the fact that no single object is anything more than labels, just names. Secondly there is the fact that, when we try to seek out the thing that got the name, we find only emptiness: that there is not a single atom of natural existence in whatever object we have chosen.

At some point you gain an ability to explain these two facts so that *they come together,* and *no longer alternate.* That is, you come to realize how both emptiness and interdependence can apply to one and the same object, with no contradiction at all.

You see then that interdependence is infallible, that it is nothing but using a concept to label the collection of parts that serve as the basis to take our label. *Just seeing* this fact, *that interdependence never fails, brings* you a *realization* that completely obviates *the way* that your tendency to grasp to true existence *holds its objects.* And then when you think of emptiness, you see interdependence; when you think of interdependence, you see emptiness. This is by the way what certain holy sages have meant when they said, "Once you grasp the secret of interdependence, the meaning of emptiness comes in a flash."[167]

Once all this happens to you, you come to realize that the point of interdependence is that nothing exists truly. And this point itself, that nothing exists truly, has the power then of bringing out in your mind a strong and certain realization that interdependence never fails. *And then* you know that the *analysis* you are performing, now *using* the pure *view* of the "Implication" section of the Middle Way school, *is* finally *complete.* We can also say, concluded our Lama, that you have then found the unique thought of Nagarjuna himself.

XVIII. A UNIQUE TEACHING
OF THE "IMPLICATION" SCHOOL

The fifth and final section in our explanation of correct
view concerns a unique teaching followed by the "Implication" group of the Middle Way school. This instruction
is contained in the following verse of the root text.

(13)

> In addition, the appearance prevents the
>   existence extreme;
> Emptiness that of non-existence, and if
> You see how emptiness shows in cause
>   and effect
> You'll never be stolen off by extreme views.

Now all the schools except for the members of the
"Implication" group hold that an understanding of the
appearance of things prevents you from falling into what
we call the "extreme of thinking things do not exist,"
while an understanding of emptiness prevents you from
falling into what is known as the "extreme of thinking
things do exist."

The position of the Implication group though is that
no particular object you can choose has any true existence, aside from merely appearing this way; and understanding this prevents you from going to the extreme of
thinking things exist—that is, exist in an ultimate way.
And because this mere appearance itself cannot exist on
its own, an understanding of emptiness prevents your
falling into the extreme of thinking things do not exist—
that is, do not exist in a conventional way.

Once something is interdependent there is no possibil-
ity for it to be anything else but something which does
not exist naturally—something which cannot stand on its
own. This is because it must then occur in dependence on
the collection of parts which serve as the basis that

receives our label. Look at the example of some feeble old man, unable to rise from his chair by himself, who must seek some other support to get up— he cannot stand on his own. Here it's a similar case: no object can stand on its own, no object can exist just naturally, so long as it must depend on any other factor.

Generally speaking, there are a great number of logical proofs that can be used when you want to establish the meaning of no self-nature. There is one though which is like the king of them all, and this is it: the "proof through interdependence." Let's say we put forth this argument to someone, and we say:

> Consider a sprout.
> It cannot exist truly,
> For it is interdependent.

Members of certain non-Buddhist schools will answer "I disagree with your reason," which is to say, "Sprouts are not interdependent." This they must say because they believe that every object in the universe is a manifestation of some primeval One.

The majority of the earlier Tibetan Buddhists fell into the extreme that we call "thinking things have stopped," for they would say that if something did not exist truly it could not exist at all. The schools from the Mind-Only on down, the group of schools known collectively as the "Functionalists," all fall into the extreme of "thinking things are permanent," for they cannot explain interdependence if they accept that nothing exists naturally. Members of the "Independent" group within the Middle Way school accept the idea of interdependence, but do not agree that if something is interdependent it cannot "exist by definition." This too is tantamount to the extreme of thinking things are permanent.

The real sages of the Middle Way school make a fourfold distinction: they say that nothing exists naturally, but not that nothing exists at all; everything exists merely by convention, but everything exists without existing naturally. The point of error for the Functionalists and those other schools is their failure to distinguish between these four: two kinds of "nothing exists" and two kinds of "everything exists."

According to the Implication system, both extremes— thinking things are permanent and thinking things have stopped—can be prevented with a single logical statement: "It cannot exist truly, because it is interdependent." The first part of the statement keeps us from the extreme of thinking things are permanent; the second, from the extreme of thinking things have stopped.

My own precious teacher, Chone Lama,[168] was always saying that both parts of the statement *each* prevent *both* of the extremes—permanence and stopping. He would explain this as follows: the literal sense of the statement's first part, "It cannot exist truly," serves to prevent the extreme of thinking things are permanent. The implication of saying that something cannot exist "truly" though is to say that, more generally, it is not non-existent; this then disallows the extreme of thinking that things have stopped. And this description, he would say, was enough for us to figure out for ourselves the process for the second part of the statement: " . . . because it is interdependent."

With this understanding we can see why the glorious Chandrakirti stated:

> Therefore this proof employing interdependence
> Cuts the net of every mistaken view.[169]

So we've shown that no object in the universe exists truly; we've given "because it's interdependent" as our reason for saying so; and we've demonstrated that these two facts can prevent one from falling into either extreme.

This too is why we see statements like the following, from *Root Wisdom:*

> Everything is right for any thing
> For which the state of emptiness is right.[170]

Or the well-known sutra lines:

> Form is emptiness,
> Emptiness form.[171]

These last lines by the way are stated to show that interdependence is itself empty, and emptiness itself interdependent. It helps your understanding of this point if you take the same pattern and read it as

> I am emptiness,
> Emptiness me.

In short, concluded our Lama, the laws of cause and effect are all totally proper for any entity which is empty of any natural existence. If you can just keep yourself from falling into the two extremes, you will make no great other blunders in your effort to develop correct view.

PRACTICE

XIX. PUT INTO PRACTICE
WHAT YOU HAVE LEARNED

WE HAVE NOW reached the last, the fourth part to our overall explanation of the actual body of the text. It consists of some strong words of encouragement—that the reader should try to recognize the truth of these instructions and then actually go and practice them. As the final verse of the root text says,

(14)

> When you've grasped as well as I the essential
>   points
> Of each of the three principal paths explained,
> Then go into isolation, my son, make mighty
> Efforts, and quickly win your ultimate wish.

This verse is a very personal instruction that Lord Tsongkapa, out of deepest feelings of love, has granted to all of us who hope to follow him. He is saying to us, "Go first and try to grasp the essential points of the three principal paths as I have explained them above; do so by listening to teachings on them over and over again.

"Then use contemplation to gain a recognition of the truth of these points; do this in retreat, staying in a state of isolation where you cut all ties to this life, and live according to the principle of having few material wants and being satisfied with whatever you have—keep your concerns and activities few. Make mighty efforts at this practice; act quickly, never lose yourself to putting off your practice; and then win, my son, the ultimate wish of all your many lifetimes."

There are profound essential points even within these words the Lord has used about essential points. The word "isolation," for example, is meant to refer to isolating

137

yourself not only on the outside—staying in some place far from the hustle and bustle of life—but within your own mind: keep your mind from making its usual intercontinental tour of the eight worldly thoughts and your thousand daily hopes and fears.[172]

"Making efforts" has its own special meaning: we don't say for example that you are "making efforts" when you are trying your hardest to do some bad deed. Real "efforts" are those you make with an enthusiasm for good.

"Your ultimate wish" in a sense really starts from now, and continues on up to the point where you become a Buddha yourself. And what the verse is saying is that you must put all your strength into winning your goal now, quickly, for you cannot be sure how many days are left in your life.

Just what does it mean to "make mighty efforts?" People like you an I can start a practice in the morning, like going into retreat to gain a special relationship with some holy being, and by the time evening comes around we begin looking for some mystical sign that the practice is having its effect—we expect by then to meet some deity face to face, or hear some voice that tells us we are going to get enlightened on such and such a date, or have some special dream or vision.

But that's not what religious practice is all about. The scriptures say that even our compassionate Teacher, the Lord Buddha, had to practice for three "countless" eons[173] before he attained the state of enlightenment. You and I then have to think to ourselves, "I am ready to spend no less than a hundred thousand lifetimes in my practice, if this is what it takes."

We must spend much time in learning, and reasoning out, and then meditating on the various Steps on the path to Buddhahood. To do this we have to set a goal for ourselves, for practicing and then fully realizing the three principal paths: we have to say, "At best, I am going to gain them in a day. If it takes me a month, I'll consider it average. But at the very least I will see that I have them within this year."

We should follow the words of Geshe Dolpa, one of the Seers of the Word, who said:

> Steps of the path! Steps of the path!
> They all come down to three short words:
> "Look far ahead,"
> "Think very big,"
> "Keep a pace."[174]

What he meant by the expression "Look for ahead" was that we should set our sights on becoming a Buddha. "Thinking big" means we should think to ourselves, "To reach my enlightenment, I'm going to practice absolutely all the paths, one by one: those of the three increasing scopes, and those of the secret teaching—the levels of creation and completion."

Now in the worldly side of things, people who know they must die within the year still make grand plans and act as if they're going to live a hundred. In the spiritual side of things, you and I are the opposite: we set our sights as low as we can when it comes to the threefold practice of learning, contemplating and meditating—even down to the few prayers we're supposedly reciting daily. We always pick out the easiest practice possible—we always think small, we think "This is about all I could manage."

But you're wrong: if you really put forth the effort, there's no question that you can even become a Buddha. As *The Bodhisattva's Life* says,

> Don't be a quitter, and think to yourself
> "How could I ever become a Buddha?"
> Those who've Gone That Way only speak
> The truth, and this is a truth they spoke:

"Even those who live as bugs,
Flies or gnats, and even germs,
Reach matchless, hard-won Buddhahood
If they really make an effort."

Here am I born as a man,
Able to tell what's right and wrong;
What's to keep me from getting enlightened
If I keep on acting an enlightened way?[175]

Therefore you should think as small as you can in your worldly work, but as BIG as you can in your spiritual.

Now the words "Keep a pace" mean that you should avoid the kind of practice where you go back and forth between making fierce efforts at it and then letting it go completely—laying around and doing nothing. You should rather keep a steady pace in the effort you give your spiritual practice: let it flow on constant, like some great river. Do anything in your power, our Lama concluded, to draw the very essence from this life of opportunity.

IN CONCLUSION

XX. THE CONCLUSION OF THE EXPLANATION

THIS BRINGS US to the last of the major divisions of the work: closing remarks that come with the conclusion of our explanation of the text. These are indicated in the colophon that appears after the last verse of the root text:

> **These instructions were imparted to Ngawang Drakpa, a friar from the Tsako district, by that very learned Buddhist monk, the glorious Lobsang Drakpa.**[176]

Now some of you, by listening and thinking carefully about the three principal paths as we've explained them above, might finally have come to some real recognition of what they mean—and you may wish to go on to the next step: meditating on these paths, so you can actually grow them in your mind. Here you will need to know the proper series of visualizations.[177]

The very first line of the root text, "I bow to all the high and holy lamas," tells us—in an indirect way—the first steps we will have to take. These will include visualizing the traditional assembly of holy beings, what we call the "Collection Field,"[178] as well as going through the practices of collecting great loads of good deeds, and purifying ourselves of our bad deeds. In short, we will have to use one of the "preliminary practice" or similar texts, related either to *Path of Bliss* or *Quick Path*.[179]

Even just in the sections there where you raise a correct motivation, you are going to have to do a complete mental review of the entire length of the path, from beginning to end. This means that you will also be giving thought to those Steps of the path where you try to recognize how valuable your life of leisure and fortune is, how hard such a life is to find, and so on. There is a very important difference here if, as you go along in the meditation, you keep your mind filled with a truly exceptional motivation—the wish to become a Buddha for every living being, the attitude of the highest scope. Then the realizations that come to you at these particular Steps will be for you paths that you merely share with people of the lesser and medium scopes, rather than the actual paths or attitudes as these people have them.[180]

When you come to the part where you go for refuge, you can use either system—the one in *Path of Bliss* and *Quick Path* or the one from the Collection Field painting related to this teaching—for visualizing the beings who are going to shelter you. There are two ways as well of picturing how the ambrosia descends from them to purify you: it can pulse or twist down along the outside of a light ray, or else flow down to you through the inside of a tube-like ray.

What the ambrosia has to purify is our past bad deeds and all the things that block our spiritual progress. The root of all these problems is the tendency we have, at the very bottom of our hearts, to cherish ourselves rather than others. Therefore you imagine all the bad deeds and blocks piled in a pitch-black lump in this same place: within your heart.

The ambrosia-light drops through your body and forces all the blackness down ahead of it. Underground, sitting below you, is the Lord of Death in the form of a huge black sow.[181] She has come because she hungers for your life, and her jaws are opened wide, pointed up, waiting. It is extremely important at this point that you imagine the blackness dropping into her open mouth—that it satisfies her fully, and that she will never again seek to harm you.

As you take your refuge, you keep your mind on the two reasons for doing so.[182] If these two feelings are for you just artificial, and forced, your refuge will be no better. But if they are true feelings, your refuge too will be true.

At the stage in your meditation where you practice the wish to become enlightened for every living being, there is a point where you imagine that you have already reached the goal, in order to help you actually do so later. Here you visualize that all the inhabitants of the universe are pure, free of any bad deeds or spiritual obstacles. The universe itself, the place which these beings inhabit, is a product of their collective deeds—and so you must imagine that it too is completely pure. This instruction is of high importance; it comes from the same source as the holy practices in the great secret traditions where you become the lord of a mystical world.

Next in the meditation you come to the practice of the "immeasurables";[183] here you must be aware that these are not just what they call the "four places of the Pure One," but rather something quite different. The compassion, for example, is not just that ordinary type: it is Great Compassion. And the loving-kindness is Great Loving-Kindness.

As for the order of the four immeasurables, it is important that you meditate first on the feeling of neutrality towards all beings; this then matches the feeling's position in the seven-part, cause-and-effect instruction for developing the wish to become a Buddha for every living being.

The next section in the meditation is the one we call the "special wish for Buddhahood."[184] It is not the wish itself, but it is very effective in furthering one's development of the wish.

Here are some notes about the next step in the meditation, where you visualize the "Collection Field." There is a magical tree at the base of the picture, a tree that gives you whatever you wish. You should imagine that it has grown from a union of your own merit and the enlightenment-wish of the beings of the assemblage.

Lord Tsongkapa, at the center of the group, is white; this symbolizes the quality he possesses and which we would like to achieve: cleaning ourselves of both kinds of obstacles—those that prevent us from reaching nirvana and those that prevent us from reaching total enlightenment.

To Lord Tsongkapa's own left is a volume of scripture, which you should visualize as the *Eight Thousand Verses* on the perfection of wisdom.[185] This is meant to symbolize the varying levels and needs that various disciples have, depending on how sharp their intellects are. These points, our Lama told us, were an oral teaching from his own teacher, the Great Tutor—the Holder of the Diamond.[186]

The volume of scripture in your meditation is speaking out loud, relating to you its contents. You should imagine that the book is talking about the very practices you are working on—renunciation, the wish to become a Buddha for all beings, and so on. Our Lama went on to give us some special instructions on the "threefold being," where we picture a holy being inside Lord Tsongkapa's heart, and yet another holy being within this being's heart.

When you visualize the teachers of what we call the "Blessings for Practice" lineage, you should follow the verses known as "Knowledge Unlocks the World".[187] Here you picture that all these figures, with the exception of the Holder of the Diamond, appear in the form of Gentle Voice. When you visualize this same lineage in the meditation from the *Offering to Lamas* manual,[188] there is a distinction of whether you involve it with the practice of the Great Seal or not.

The tutelary deities and similar beings in the visualization are pictured according to *Path of Bliss* and *Quick Path*. This means that in front you have those who belong to the group of secret teachings known as the "Unsurpassed." To the center figure's own right are those of the "Master Practitioner" group; to the rear are those of the "Activity" group, and to the left those of the "Action" group.[189]

You can do this visualization another way too. Picture the divine being known as "Secret Collection" at the front. On the central figure's right is "Frightener," on the left is "Highest Bliss," and at the back is "Lo Diamond," or the like. Outside of them then come deities of the Master Practitioner group, and outside of them those of the Activity group, then the Action group, and so on.[190]

There are three different ways of visualizing the crystal bath house when you come to the part where you imagine that you are washing the body of each of the holy beings as an offering to him. You can make a house appear in each of the four directions, or to the east, or else to the south. At this point you see yourself sending out copies of yourself, so that three of you stand before each member of the assembly. The act of emanating out many bodies of yourself here and at other places in the meditation has an additional benefit: it serves to ripen the potential in you of actually learning to emanate yourself. You will gain this ability when you reach the various bodhisattva levels, and use it for the good of others.

When you get to the final preliminary practice, the supplication, you should use mainly the text of "Knowledge Unlocks the World." It's permissible here if you wish to picture the central figure with a "body mandala"—a complete secret world and its inhabitants, all part of his own body. Use the one that you find in the *Offering to Lamas.*[191]

For all the other parts of the meditation—whether they relate to preliminaries, to the main meditation itself, or to its proper conclusion—you should refer to the various texts on the Steps of the path to Buddhahood and apply the appropriate sections. It is very good if, at the very conclusion of your meditation session, you can recite a closing prayer starting with the line, "May this good deed, standing for whatever ones are done . . ."[192]

I have been fortunate enough, our Lama concluded, to receive these instructions on the *Three Principal Paths*—on both the verses of the text and their commentary—at the feet of many saintly, accomplished sages. I heard them from the holy lips of my own precious Lama, my protector and savior, who is the lord of the wish to achieve Buddhahood for all beings, and who was one and the same with the savior Serlingpa.[193] And I heard them from my refuge and lord, the Holder of the Diamond from Drupkang, whose blessed name my lips are hardly worthy to pronounce: the good and glorious Lobsang Ngawang Tenzin Gyatso.

I have tried here to offer you but a very brief teaching on the three principal paths, using the lines of the root text as our guide. I beseech every person here, please be so very kind, as to take what I have offered in my words and put it into actual practice, to the absolute best that you can.

Thus did our Lama bless us, and with joy then uttered the verse with which we dedicate a great good deed, to the good of every living being.[194]

PRAYER

XXI. A DISCIPLE'S PRAYER

HE'S THE LORD who stages and then withdraws the
    show, a myriad *ocean*
Of *mighty deeds* the Victors in all three times
    perform to *keep*
The teaching tradition that joins both ways,
    those passed from Gentle Voice
And from the savior *Loving One,* the deep thought
    of the Victors.[195]

He's a god who goes to the matchless mystery
    of his mind, a treasure
Resplendent with all ten forces, to speak
    the gold mine of the sages;
He's Lobsang Drakpa, of shining fame, and
    into this world came
The jewels of the holy dharma spewed out
    from his lips.[196]

He's the revered father of all Victors; in the
    form of their son, a child,[197]
Gave a teaching that draws the essence of
    the nectar from the cream
Of the eighty thousand,[198] the mystery of
    the Buddhas' speech: we call it
Three Principal Paths, well-known as the sun
    in the sky of the immaculate Word.

His lines are none of those empty words,
    supposedly deep, incomplete,
But rather spout a thousand riches, advice
    from experience
Of each step of the meaning itself, the
    high paths in their entirety,
Capturing the glory of good of the world
    or peace, wherever.[199]

Come great warrior, who has no fear of what
    will make him wise;
Take up the bow of these wonderful books, the
    true Word, open and secret;
Use it with the feathered shafts of reasoning,
    way of the wise
Throughout the world, pierce the hearts of
    those who would teach wrong.

When will I decide to give the rest of my
    life some meaning?
When will I throw away this lie of
    happiness in this life,
The shining embrace of grabbing after
    good things in this world,
My forever friend, the foe of my
    forever happiness.

In this and my future lives may I never
    fail to collect
More of the short and long-term causes
    which bring me both the bodies;[200]
May I win the beauty of eyes that guide
    myself and others too
On the excellent paths, fixed upon
    the wise and adept ahead.

This is not a load that the likes of me
    could ever bear,
But I've tried my best to put his eloquence
    down in black and white.
I may have slipped, and lost some words
    or meaning, or the like;
I kneel before my Lama and freely admit
    any errors made.

By the pure white force in deeds like this
    endeavor I've completed
May my thoughts, those of others too, all turn

to the holy dharma.
May it come to cause us all to cut what
  ties us to this life,
And help us take best essence from the time
  and chance we have.

So this is the teaching on the three principal paths given
by our lord and lama, the one who granted us all three
kinds of kindness,[201] our savior, the god who stood at the
center of our universe, the Holder of the Diamond himself, the good and glorious Pabongka. He bestowed upon
us many times this profound instruction, using the words
of the root text as a guide.

Various records were made on the different occasions
that he delivered this teaching; there were five such man-
uscripts in the hands of different people. They have been
compiled here by myself, Suddhi Vadzra,[202] a monk from
the monastery of Den, a man who ails from his lack of
spiritual knowledge, a mere pretender dressed in robes,
the very lowest of the whole great circle of disciples who
have reverently bowed and touched their heads at the
holy dust upon the feet of the great Lama, our dear
father, whose kindness defies repayment.

I was able to complete this work because of the blessings of this highest of guides himself; those received during the many years I spent at his side while he was living,
and those which even now emanate from his remains, his
precious relics.

I have written these pages where those relics themselves reside, bathed in the light that blazes from them,
at that holy hermitage known as Tashi Chuling.[203]

May it help all living beings!

A SECRET KEY

XXII. A SECRET KEY
TO THE THREE PRINCIPAL PATHS

HERE IS A "Secret Key to the Three Principal Paths," consisting of notes composed by Gungtang.[204]

The opening line of Lord Tsongkapa's *Three Principal Paths,* what we call the "offering of praise," is meant to indicate the root of all successful practice—proper reliance on a spiritual teacher—and the six preliminaries.[205]

The lines including the one that reads "The essence of all high teachings of the Victors" can be taken as applying to the three principal paths individually, or to the three as a whole. When you teach someone these three paths, you go through them one by one; but when you meditate upon them, each one must be suffused with the other two. This fact you can ascertain from the introductory reference to the latter two paths in the very first verse. If you didn't do your meditations this way, then your feelings of renunciation could not be considered a path of the greater way.

Everyone gets the urge from time to time to do some spiritual practice, but all of us are cheated of the chance by our tendency to put our practice off for another day. This is why, in the root text, Lord Tsongkapa gives the teaching on this precious life of opportunity right together with the advices on our approaching death.

He also juxtaposes the teaching on the problems of cyclic life and the teaching on actions and their consequences—for the reason that every pain we feel in this circle of life is caused by the bad deeds we have done before.

In the verses where he explains how to meditate on the wish for enlightenment too he manages to interweave both systems—the one taught by Lord Atisha and the one which Master Shantideva gave. The fact that the word "mothers" in these verses is plural is meant to refer to the one system, where you exchange you self-concern with a concern for others—a kind of even-mindedness.[206] The very mention of the word "mother" at all is meant to refer to the step in the other system where you recognize that all beings are your own mother. And the words that come before the mention of "mothers" are meant to bring out the step of compassion.

When you "think of what's happening"[207] here you can do it two ways. You can *think of what* other beings did for you in the past when they were your mothers; this is how you remember their kindness in the step that follows recognizing them as mothers in the first place, in the one system. On top of that you can also *think of what* other beings are doing for you even now, every day; this is how it's done in the system where you exchange yourself and others. This second way of doing it gives fantastic results: you no longer have to worry that you lost your chance to plant this fertile field by repaying their kindness then, for here they are around you, lots of fields to plant. It's only your own failure to recognize their present kindness; they are your ticket to fulfilling the needs of every living being, but you don't give them any credit for it.

Now the concept of interdependence can refer to the fact that things come from causes. Sometimes though things can be turned all upside down, like spears that you plant points-up to support a canopy, and we can say in many cases that "causes" depend on "results." Therefore the system that we use here is based principally on inter-dependence in the sense of labelling due to dependence.

How does the labelling work? Suppose there's a person who never had the name "Tashi," and then one day you go and give him the new name "Tashi."[208] After a few days you begin to forget that it was you who gave him the name "Tashi," and he starts looking like he is "Tashi" all on his own. The process by which your perception changes here is rather subtle and difficult to recognize. You can read all the books and start to think you know what no-self is, but then you've got to go back to the lower school systems and work your way up: make sure you can picture what they think "no-self" means as well. If you can't then you're probably pretty far from correct view yourself.[209]

Here in his verses Lord Tsongkapa first makes the statement that, unless you have the wisdom that perceives ultimate reality, the other two principal paths can never free you. Then the next thing he mentions, at least directly, is interdependence. The point he is trying to make is "If you understand interdependence, you understand ultimate reality; if not, then you don't."

And the same can be said for grasping the fact that an understanding of the appearance of things prevents you from falling into the extreme of thinking things exist. Even a non-Buddhist school like the so-called "Cast-Offs"[210] can think the opposite: not even they make the mistake of denying that understanding the appearance of things prevents you from falling into the extreme of thinking that nothing exists. Therefore the idea that it keeps you from falling into the first extreme is truly unique.

The above are only a few words of instruction, but they represent the concentrated essence of everything that the Master Tutor, the Precious One, has taught. Hold them therefore very dear to your heart.

The original woodblock printing of this text was sponsored by a devotee of matchless faith and morals, from the house of Hlalu, a veritable garden of bliss.[211] He dedicates this act to the higher good of every living being.

NOTES

1 *illustrious scholar Changkya Rolpay Dorje:* An excellent introduction to the history of the Changkya line has been written by E. Gene Smith and is included in his foreword to the collected works of the Tibetan sage Tuken Dharma Vajra (see pp. 1–7, vol. 1, bibliography entry 52).

2 *fifteen scroll-paintings:* There are at least four sets of the paintings outside of Tibet; they are very much alike because the "paintings" are actually block-prints. In my student days these prints were available at Narthang Monastery near the town of Shigatse to the southwest of Lhasa—one would hire a painter to fill in the colors and write the traditional inscriptions explaining each scene.

3 *I don't see how . . .* See pp. 221–2 of Vol. I of the Rinpoche's biography, bibliography entry 55.

4 *Ngawang Drakpa and his classmates:* See p. 293, bibliography entry 27.

5 *famous bodhisattva Ever-Weeping:* The text is still extant; see bibliography entry 64.

6 *these few beautiful lines:* The lines quoted by Pabongka Rinpoche's biographer appear on p. 584 (bibliography entry 69). Immediately following this letter in Lord Tsongkapa's collected works are preserved two more sent to Ngawang Drakpa; the first of these contains the *Three Principal Paths*.

7 *Door to the Noble Path:* The edition of Pabongka Rinpoche's commentary translated here is listed at bibliography entry 46; the original verses by Lord Tsongkapa are found in his collected works at entry 68. Some other useful explanations of Lord Tsongkapa's *Three Principal Paths* are those by the following masters:

> The Great Fifth Dalai Lama, Ngawang Lobsang
>   Gyatso (1617–1682) at entries 16 and 17;
> Tsechok Ling, Yeshe Gyeltsen (1713–1793) at
>   entries 78 and 79;

Tendar Hlarampa (b. 1759) at entry 30;
Welmang Konchok Gyeltsen (1764–1853) at
   entry 7;
Ngulchu Dharmabhadra (1772–1851) at entries
   37 and 38; as well as
Mokchok Trulku (modern) at entry 59.

8 *Holder of the Diamond:* A form of the Buddha in which he gives secret teachings.

9 *the saffron robe:* The robes of a human, Buddhist monk.

10 *secret three of every Victor:* The mystery of body, speech, and mind of every one of the countless Buddhas. Buddhas are called "Victors" because they have overcome the obstacles that prevent one from eliminating all bad thoughts and knowing all things.

11 *Gentle Voice:* Divine form representing all the wisdom of the Buddhas.

12 *Three Principal Paths:* "Path" in Buddhist philosophy refers to a stage of mental realization. The title has often been translated as "Three Principles of the Path," but the point is that renunciation, the wish for enlightenment, and correct view are each one a principal path.

13 *Dharma:* A word of many meanings, most often "spiritual teachings" or "existing object."

14 *all three realms:* Meaning all the world. Buddhism teaches that there are three realms of existence. We live in the "desire" realm, so called because our principal interests are food and sex. Higher up is the "form" realm, where beings live in a state of meditation and have beautiful forms. Even higher is the "formless" realm, where beings are free of gross suffering and have only mental bodies.

15 *More than a wishing jewel . . .* From the very brief version of Lord Tsongkapa's *Steps on the Path to Buddhahood* (f. 56a, bibliography entry 63). The entire context appears below in the discussion of renunciation.

16 *three "problems of the pot":* How not to listen to a teaching—like a pot with the lid closed (not paying attention to what is going on), a pot full of grime (listening with ignoble motivations, such as the desire for a big repu-

tation), and a pot with the bottom fallen out (not retaining what was heard—one is advised to review daily with one's fellow students). See Lord Tsongkapa's greater *Steps on the Path*, entry 61, f. 16; as well as Pabongka Rinpoche's famed *Liberation in Our Hands*, entry 47, ff. 54–5.

17 *six images for the instruction:* How one should listen to a teaching—

    a) Think of yourself as a patient, for your
        mental afflictions (desire and the rest)
        make you sick.

    b) Think of the dharma as medicine.

    c) Think of your teacher as a master physician.

    d) Think of following his teachings exactly,
        and as long as needed, as following the
        doctor's orders to get better.

    e) Think of the Buddhas as infallible, or of
        the Infallible One (your teacher) as a
        Buddha.

    f) Pray that this great cure, the teachings
        of the Buddhas, may long remain in the
        world.

See Lord Tsongkapa, entry 61, ff. 16–19, and Pabongka Rinpoche, entry 47, ff. 55–61.

18 *three lands:* That is, below the earth (where the serpent-beings and similar creatures live), upon the earth (where men are found), and in the sky above the earth (where deities make their home).

19 *Ngawang Drakpa:* See the Foreword for a description of this disciple's life.

20 *three different scopes:* The wish to escape oneself from the lower realms, the wish to escape oneself from the entire circle of life, and the wish to achieve full enlightenment for the sake of every living being.

21 *lives of misery:* A birth in the hells, as an insatiable spirit, or as an animal.

22 *Channels and Winds, etc.:* All highly advanced practices from the secret teachings of the Buddha.

23 *Geshe Puchungwa (1031–1106) and Chen-ngawa (1038–1103):* Source of quotation not found. Geshe Puchungwa, full name Shunnu Gyeltsen, was one of the "three great brothers," direct disciples of Lord Drom Tonpa who helped him found and spread the Seer tradition of the early Tibetan Buddhist masters (see notes 36 and 49 below). Chen-ngawa, also known as Tsultrim Bar, was another of the three, as was the great Potowa (see note 42).

24 *five sciences:* Classical grammar, logic, Buddhist theory, the fine arts, and medicine.

25 *five types of clairvoyance:* Supernormal powers of emanation, sight, hearing, perception of the past, and knowledge of others' thoughts.

26 *eight great attainments:* These are to gain "the sword," which allows one to travel anywhere; "the pill," which enables you to become invisible or assume any outer form; "the eye ointment," which helps you see minute or very distant objects; "swift feet," the ability to travel at high speeds; "taking essence," an ability to live off nothing but tiny bits of sustenance; "sky walk," the ability to fly; "disappearing" or invisibility; and "underground," the power to pass through solid ground like a fish through water.

27 *Lord Atisha (982–1054):* Full name Dipamkara Shri Jnyana, illustrious Indian sage who brought the teachings of the Steps of the path to Tibet. Author of *Lamp on the Path,* a prototype text of this genre (bibliography entry 57).

28 *the Brahmin's son Tsanakya:* In his classic work on the Steps to Buddhahood, Pabongka Rinpoche explains that Tsanakya was able to master the difficult secret practice of the Lord of Death, but fell to the lowest hell because he used his knowledge to harm other beings (f. 225b, entry 47).

29 *master meditator of Lo Diamond:* The Rinpoche's *Liberation in Our Hands* again explains (f. 291b, entry 47). The practitioner undertook one of the most powerful practices of the secret teachings, but due to his less than perfect

motivation was able to achieve only a lower result. Lord Atisha notes here that such practitioners had even dropped to the hells.

30 *giving, morality, etc.*: The first five of the six Buddhist perfections. The last is the perfection of wisdom.

31 *Suppose you fail* . . . Quotation from Lord Tsongkapa's report to his teacher and disciple, the venerable Rendawa, on teachings received from Gentle Voice himself (ff. 2b-3a, entry 62).

32 *body of form and dharma body:* The physical form of a Buddha and his mind (along with this mind's ultimate nature) are called the "form body" and "dharma body," respectively.

33 *two obstacles:* See note 10.

34 *two types of desire to reach Buddhahood:* See note 136.

35 *Suppose you try* . . . Quotation from Lord Tsongkapa's *opus magnum* (f. 156b, entry 61).

36 *Everybody's got some mystic being* . . . Original source of quotation not found; it appears also in Pabongka Rinpoche's *Liberation in Our Hands* (f. 294a, entry 47). The Seers of the Word were an eminent group of early Buddhist masters in Tibet whose lineage descended from Lord Atisha and his principal disciple, Lord Drom Tonpa. The school's name in Tibetan, "Kadampa," is explained as meaning that they were able to see the Word of the Buddha *(ka)* as personal instruction *(dam)* that applied immediately to their own practice.

37 *I used the "Lamp on the Path":* The full context of this quotation appears in Pabongka Rinpoche's *Liberation in Our Hands* (f. 37b, entry 47); it reveals much of the sources of our text and restates its comprehensive nature. Lord Tsongkapa has just related the contents of a major section of his massive *Greater Steps on the Path to Buddhahood* to his divine mentor, Gentle Voice. And then,

Gentle Voice asked the Lord in a playful way, "Well now, is there anything in your work that isn't covered in those three principal paths I taught you?"

Lord Tsongkapa replied, "This is how I composed my work. I took the three principal paths which you, oh Holy One, taught me, and made them the very life of the path. I used the *Lamp on the Path* as my basic text, and supplemented it with many other advices of the Seers of the Word."

38 *Master Dandin:* Hindu poet dated to about the 7th Century A.D., author of *The Mirror of Poetics,* a renowned treatise on composition (quotation on f. 322b, entry 34). The brief quotation that follows next in the text is from an immense treatise written by the Indian sage Shakyabuddhi in explanation of Master Dharmakirti's *Commentary on Valid Perception* (see f. 1a, first volume of entry 82A, and note 133 below).

39 *traditions of "far-reaching activity" and "profound view":* Refer, respectively, to the teachings on the wish for enlightenment and correct view (the former assuming renunciation, the third principal path). See also note 195.

40 *"Knowledge Unlocks the World":* Famed verses of supplication by Lord Tsongkapa himself, named from the opening line (see f. 3a, entry 65). The three beings mentioned are different forms of the Buddha.

41 *three types of knowledge:* Realizations of the true nature of reality, in varying degrees.

42 *To reach liberation . . .* Geshe Potowa (1031–1105), full name Rinchen Sel, was a master of the Seer tradition and one of the three great disciples of Lord Drom Tonpa (see notes 23 and 49). His *Metaphors* (with commentary at entry 19) are an important predecessor to later works on the Steps. The quotation here is found on p. 14 of Hladri Gangpa's commentary to the *Blue Book* (see entry 89), a compilation of the great Potowa's teachings written out by his student Geshe Dolpa (see note 174).

43 *source of good qualities:* Opening words of a supplication from a famed devotional text, the *Offering to Lamas,* by the venered Lobsang Chukyi Gyeltsen, first of the illustrious Panchen Lamas of Tibet (p. 54, entry 51). The three verses mentioned here read as follows:

> Source of all good qualities, great sea
> of morality;

Brimming with a mass of jewels, teachings
   you have learned;
My lord, second Lord of the Able, wearing
   a saffron robe;
I seek your blessing, master who keeps
   the knowledge of the vows.

You who have all ten qualities that one
   must possess to be
Worthy to teach the path of all those
   who have gone to bliss;
Lord of the dharma, regent standing in
   for every Victor;
I seek your blessing, spiritual guide
   for the greater way.

All three gateways well restrained, wise,
   and patient, and straight;
Free of guile, deception; learned in
   the secrets and their texts;
Master at writing and edifying two tens
   of secret lore;
I seek your blessing, first among all of
   those who hold the diamond.

"Lord of the Able" refers to the present Buddha; the "ten qualities" are listed in the verse directly following.

44 *steady and wise:* A Buddhist monk is "steady" when he has kept his vows pure for at least ten years following his ordination. "Wise" refers to knowledge of a whole list of subjects in the study of ethics, such as understanding what is a moral downfall and what is not, or which misdeeds are more serious than others.

45 *the three trainings:* These are exceptional morality, exceptional concentration, and exceptional wisdom.

46 *Jewel of the Sutras:* A "sutra" is an open teaching of the Buddha. The verse is from a famed commentary taught to Master Asanga (c. 350 A.D.) by Loving One, the Future Buddha (ff. 20a-20b, entry 43).

47 *eight great benefits:* The eight are described as coming close to Buddhahood, pleasing the Buddhas, overcoming

evil influences, avoiding improper activities and thoughts, reaching high realizations, always meeting teachers, never falling to the lower realms, and attaining temporary and ultimate goals with ease (Lord Tsongkapa, entry 61, ff. 33–6; Pabongka Rinpoche, entry 47, ff. 124–9).

48 *First then see* . . . Again, quoted from the briefer version of his *Steps on the Path* (f. 56a, entry 63).

49 *the great Drom Tonpa (1005–1064):* Full name Gyalway Jungne, most famed disciple of Lord Atisha, himself the great progenitor of the teaching on the Steps in Tibet. Founded the renowned Radreng Monastery in central Tibet. The *Blue Annals* relate how he gained miraculous powers after clearing Lord Atisha's excrement off the floor of the Master's cell (p. 259, entry 94). Lord Atisha himself, it is said, took a perilous journey by sea for over a year to meet one of his principal teachers in what is now Indonesia. After arriving, he examined his teacher for some time before becoming his student, and then served him for twelve years.

50 *Lord Milarepa (1040–1123):* The famed cave-meditator of Tibet, author of some of the greatest spiritual poetry in any language (several examples appear below in the section on renunciation). The hardships he undertook as a test from his teacher Marpa are famous; see for example the *Blue Annals,* entry 94, pp. 430–1.

51 *Marpa (1012–1097) and Naropa (1016–1100):* Marpa, also known as the "Great Translator," was a teacher of Lord Milarepa and an early Tibetan Buddhist who helped bring the secret teachings from India. His own teacher was Naropa, a renowned Indian master who also instructed Lord Atisha. As Pabongka Rinpoche again relates in his *Liberation in Our Hands* (f. 133a, entry 47), Marpa was once faced with the choice of prostrating first to his teacher or to a fantastic divine being who had made his appearance in the room; he made the mistake of selecting the latter. Milarepa's offering to Marpa himself is mentioned on the same folio.

52 *throneholder Tenpa Rabgye and the master tutor Ngawang Chujor:* Lobsang Yeshe Tenpa Rabgye, also known as

Achi Tuno Monhan, was a distinguished scholar of the Gelukpa tradition of Tibetan Buddhism; his title indicates that he held the throne passed down from Lord Tsongkapa himself. His collected works—chiefly on the secret teachings—are still extant in two volumes (entry 32). From the colophons of these works we learn that he did most of his writing at Ganden Monastery near Lhasa, and seems to have been born about 1758. Here he also states that he learned about the two forms of the wish for enlightenment chiefly from the great Ngawang Chujor.

53 *Sakya Pandita (1182–1251):* Full name Kunga Gyeltsen, one of the greatest spiritual teachers of all Central Asia, renowned translator and commentator of the Buddhist canon, brought the tradition from Tibet to the Mongolians. Venerable Drak-gyen (full name Drakpa Gyeltsen, 1147–1216) was his uncle and mentor; see also note 86 below.

54 *A person who doesn't treat as a lama . . .* The quotation is found on f. 161b (entry 82) of a commentary on the secret teaching of the Lord of Death composed by Ratnakara Shanti, also known as Shantipa. He was a famed master of the great Vikramashila Monastery in northeast India during the 10th Century, and taught Lord Atisha before his journey to Tibet.

55 *Wheel of Time:* Original source for the quotation not found; it appears in Pabongka Rinpoche's great work on the Steps of the path (f. 130b, entry 47), attributed only to the "Wheel of Time" with no mention of "root text." The root text for the secret teaching on the Wheel of Time was huge, twelve thousand verses long, and only abridgements have been included in the Tibetan canon. See entry 24 for the principal version.

56 *the greater way:* The Buddha gave various levels of teachings for disciples of different capacities; these are known as the "greater" and "lesser" ways.

57 *Fifty Verses on Lamas:* Traditional manual on how to behave towards one's spiritual guide, by the great Buddhist poet Ashvaghosha (c. 100 A.D.). The thirteen causes of a premature death are listed on f. 10a (entry 29) and

explained by Lord Tsongkapa in his commentary (pp. 334–6, entry 66) as follows: an unbearable pain in the skull, injury by various powerful animals, different illnesses, demonic forces, plague, poison, authorities of the land, fire, snakes, water, spirits, thieves, and fierce demigods. After dying in one of these ways, the person descends directly to the hells.

58 *the master Sangye Yeshe:* In his masterpiece on the Steps to Buddhahood (f. 132a, entry 47), Pabongka Rinpoche relates the story of how the Indian master Sangye Yeshe (not to be confused with the later Tibetan savant of the same name) was delivering a teaching when he spotted his tutor passing by. This was the great Paktsangwa, whose name means "Swineherd," for he was posing as a common pig farmer. Sangye Yeshe pretended not to notice his lama, so he would not have to pay the pig herder obeisance before his assembled students. He later swore to his teacher that he had not seen him, and as a result his eyes fell from their sockets. The account is also mentioned in passing by Sonam Hlay Wangpo in his book of illustrations for the *Heap of Jewel Metaphors* (p. 172, entry 88).

59 *disciple of Geshe Neusurpa:* Pabongka Rinpoche, on the same folio as the preceding note, somewhat elucidates by saying that the disciple had failed in his pledges to his teacher and so showed great terror at the moment of his death; the disciple's name is not mentioned. Geshe Neusurpa, full name Yeshe Bar (1042–1118), was one of the early Seer masters of Tibetan Buddhism; he studied under Potowa and other great teachers, and counted among his many disciples the illustrious Langri Tangpa Dorje Senge, author of the popular *Mental Training in Eight Verses*.

60 *the Buddha himself:* A number of such declarations by the Buddha himself that one's lama is the Buddha himself are quoted by Lord Tsongkapa himself in his greater work on the Steps (see f. 29*ff.*, entry 61).

61 *Sakya, Geluk, and Nyingma:* Names of three of the lineages that developed in Tibet for passing on the Buddha's

teachings. The Geluk tradition began with Lord Tsongkapa himself.

62 *Every high teaching* . . . Textual source not located. Gungtang Jampeyang (1762–1823), also known as Gungtang Konchok Tenpay Dronme, was a student of the first reincarnation of the great Jamyang Shepa (see the Foreword and entry 27). He is known for his eloquent spiritual poetry and philosophical works; his incisive comments on the *Three Principal Paths* have been appended to the edition of Pabongka Rinpoche's commentary used for the present translation, and are included in the final section.

63 *I have come to the realization* . . . Lord Tsongkapa's letter to his teacher is still extant; the quoted lines appear on f. 69b (entry 67). The name "Dipamkara Jnyana" refers to Lord Atisha.

64 *the three collections:* Three principal divisions of the Buddha's teachings: the collection of vowed morality (which concerns principally the training on morality), the collection of sutra (principally the training of concentration), and the collection of knowledge (the training of wisdom).

65 *an abbreviated abbreviation* . . . Again, from the very brief version of Lord Tsongkapa's *Steps on the Path to Buddhahood* (f. 56a, entry 63).

66 *His wondrous word* . . . Source of quotation not found. See note 49 for the author's background.

67 *three distinguishing features and four greatnesses:* The three features that distinguish the teaching on the Steps from other instructions are that it includes all the subjects of both the open and secret teachings, is easily put to practice, and has come down to us through masters of the two great traditions described in note 195 (Pabongka Rinpoche, entry 47, ff. 48b-50b; Lord Tsongkapa, entry 61, f. 8b). The four greatnesses of the teaching are that one comes to realize all the teachings as consistent, one perceives all the scriptures as personal advice, one easily grasps the true intent of the Buddhas (none other than the three principal paths), and one automatically avoids the Great

Mistake of disparaging any teaching (Lord Tsongkapa, entry 61, ff. 8b-14b; Pabongka Rinpoche, entry 47, ff. 41b-48b).

68 *the glorious Secret Collection:* One of the major secret teachings of the Buddha (entry 87).

69 *Jewel of Realizations:* Important text on the perfection of wisdom imparted to Master Asanga by Loving One; refer to note 46 (entry 44).

70 *Try to mix up all the systems . . .* Source of quotation not found. Tuken Dharma.Vajra, also known as Lobsang Chukyi Nyima (1737–1802), was the third of the Tuken line of spiritual masters and is famed for his work on comparative Buddhist school systems, as well as for biographies of saints such as Changkya Rolpay Dorje, said to be the former life of Pabongka Rinpoche himself (see the Foreword, and also his collected works at entry 52).

71 *royal lama Jangchub Uw:* 11th Century ruler of the Guge kingdom of western Tibet, instrumental in bringing Lord Atisha and his teachings to the Land of Snows.

72 *It is this perfection . . .* The wording of the sutra as found in the Tibetan canon differs slightly, although the intent is the same (f. 206a, entry 84).

73 *Even in some insignificant business . . .* Quotation from f. 95a of his famed work on the three types of vows (entry 2, see also note 53).

74 *The point: if you don't meditate . . .* Source of quotation not found. See note 50 for information on its author.

75 *the sage Kyungpo Neljor (978–1079):* His persistence in seeking the secret traditions in India and bringing them to Tibet is well documented in the *Blue Annals* (pp. 728*ff.,* entry 94). Bon is the shamanistic religion which was prevalent in Tibet prior to the introduction of Buddhism.

76 *Sakya lama Kun-nying (1092–1158):* Full name Kunga Nyingpo, son of the founder of the famed Sakya Monastery in north-central Tibet, and grandfather of the illustrious Sakya Pandita (see note 53).

77 *The renunciation of all three . . .* From a work in the

secret teachings devoted to Gentle Voice (quotation from f. 10a, entry 25).

78 *Master Dandin:* Refer to the word "essence" back in his verse explained at note 38.

79 *We call someone . . .* From a classic text on the teachings of emptiness by Master Aryadeva (c. 200 A.D.). Quotation from f. 13a, entry 40.

80 *six images for the instruction:* For these and the three "problems of the pot," see notes 16 and 17.

81 *the first one of these verses:* The greater "Steps on the Path" treats the eminence of the author on folios 3a-8a, and the eminence of the teaching on folios 8a-14b. Advice on how to teach and learn the steps is found on folios 14b-22a. The actual instructions on how to lead students along the Steps of the path comprise folios 22a-523a. These four basic sections are found in the middle-length version of the "Steps on the Path" at folios 2a-5b; folios 5b-8b; folios 8b-13b; and folios 13b-201b. Both works are by Lord Tsongkapa (see entries 61 and 60, respectively).

82 *normal suffering being:* Our being consists of our physical form, our feelings, our ability to discriminate, our remaining mental functions and various other parts, and our consciousness. These are known as the "heaps," or groups of things that make us up, since each of the five divisions involves numerous members piled together. They are "impure" basically because they are products of and also promote bad thoughts and ignorant actions.

83 *lower nirvana:* Nirvana, or the permanent end of all one's mental afflictions, is equivalent to Buddhahood if one attains it with the wish to liberate all beings. Nirvana without this wish is a "lower nirvana."

84 *About this attitude . . .* Quotation found on ff. 168a-168b of Lord Tsongkapa's *Greater Steps on the Path* (entry 61). Sharawa (1070–1141) was one of the pillars of the early Seer tradition of Tibetan Buddhist masters; he was a student of the great Potowa and a teacher of the illustrious Chekapa.

85 *Only in Tibet . . .* Original source not found. The quota-

tion also appears in the greater work on the Steps by Lord Tsongkapa (f. 206b, entry 61).

86 *No practitioner, a person who loves this life . . .* Quotation from p. 436 of this classic "mental training" text of the venerable Drakpa Gyeltsen (entry 12, see also note 53). The "four loves" are listed this way:

> Love for this life, which makes one
> no practitioner.
> Love for this world, which is no
> renunciation.
> Love for one's selfish interests, which
> makes one no bodhisattva.
> Grasping to a real "me," which is no
> correct view.

87 *repeated three times, and loud:* A full account of the incident is found in the *Collected Sayings of the Seers,* compiled by Tsunpa Chegom; see f. 21, entry 18. For information on Lord Drom Tonpa, see note 49.

88 *Shang Nachung Tonpa:* The incident with Lord Atisha is related by Lord Tsongkapa in his *Greater Steps on the Path* (f. 192a, entry 61); similar exchanges appear in Pabongka Rinpoche's *Liberation* (ff. 169a and 294a, entry 47) and in the *Collected Sayings of the Seers* (f. 5b, entry 18). We read in the *Blue Annals* that this student was himself a master of the teachings of Loving One, the Future Buddha, and imparted them to Monton Jung-ne Sherab, a nephew of the renowned translator Ma Lotsawa (pp. 232–3, entry 94).

89 *They go into seclusion . . .* Source of this and the following quotation not found. Both appear in Pabongka Rinpoche's *Liberation in Our Hands* (f. 171a, entry 47). "Droway Gonpo" is a name applied to a number of Tibetan sages; Pabongka Rinpoche adds the word "Gyer" before the name in one instance, but it is still not clear to whom the quotations are to be attributed.

90 *All the spiritual practice . . .* Original source of quotation not found. Ngari Panchen, full name Padma Wan-

gyal (1487–1543), was a sage of the Nyingma tradition of Tibetan Buddhism.

91 *Oh worldly wise!* From the famed epistle of spiritual instruction sent by the great Buddhist philosopher Master Nagarjuna (c. 200 A.D.) to the Indian king Udayibhadra (f. 42a, entry 6; for English translation see p. 68, entry 95).

92 *In the city of daily concerns . . .* Original source of quotation not found; the lines appear as well in Pabongka Rinpoche's work on the Steps (f. 169b, entry 47). It is a practice for Buddhist meditators to go to some frightening place, like a cemetery or a high cliff, to observe their heightened sense of a "self" and better understand it. Graveyards in Tibet and India were especially fear-inspiring because bodies were simply laid out rather than buried, and this would attract dangerous wild animals. The great Lingrepa, full name Padma Dorje (1128–1188), was a student of Droway Gonpo Pakmo Drupa and founded one of the orders of the Kagyu tradition of Tibetan Buddhism.

93 *It doesn't do any good . . .* The quotation is found, fittingly, in his treatise on the secret practice of "great completion" (p. 221, entry 76). Yang Gonpa, full name Gyal Tsen Pel (1213–1258), and his teacher Gu-tsangpa Gonpo Dorje (1189–1258) were also founding fathers of one of the orders of the Kagyu tradition.

94 *ten "ultimate riches":* We see the roots of these ten riches in the instructions of Geshe Shawopa among the *Collected Sayings of the Seers* (ff. 47b-48b, entry 18).

95 *And in the days when my teaching . . .* The Buddha's eloquent oath appears on f. 414, entry 28. The "saffron robe" is that of a Buddhist monk.

96 *In future days . . .* Source of this and following quotation not located.

97 *Gyalchok Kelsang Gyatso (1708–1757) and Panchen Lobsang Yeshe (1663–1737):* The former was the seventh of the Dalai Lamas, spiritual and temporal rulers of Tibet. He built the Norbulingka, magnificent summer palace of the

Dalai Lamas, and sponsored a carving of the wooden printing-blocks for the entire collection of over 4,000 titles in the Tibetan Buddhist canon. The latter figure was the second of the Panchen Lamas, another exalted lineage of spiritual and temporal leaders centered at the great Tashi Lhunpo Monastery in south-central Tibet. He was an eminent practitioner and scholar of Buddhism while still one of the most powerful political figures of his time.

98 *relinquished their thrones and left the home:* The Buddha himself turned down the opportunity to become a World Emperor, and was originally Prince Siddhartha, son of King Suddhodana and Queen Maya of the vast Shakya empire of north India. Master Shantideva, the great 8th Century Buddhist philosopher and poet, was born son of the king of Saurashtra, in what is now Gujarat (north of Bombay). Lord Atisha was the son of King Kalyanashri and Queen Prabhavati, rulers of the 10th Century Sahor kingdom of Bengal, around Calcutta; their might was said to equal that of the Emperor of China.

99 *the emperor of China:* The incident occurred in 1408, and the emissaries were dispatched by Yung Lo, the third emperor of the Ming Dynasty. In his stead, Lord Tsongkapa sent Jamchen Chuje Shakya Yeshe, who later went on to found the great Sera Monastery, where Pabongka Rinpoche was himself trained nearly 500 years later. The "Purest Eight" who followed the Master into retreat were Jamkarwa Jampel Chusang, Neten Sangkyongwa, Neten Rinchen Gyeltsen, Neten Jangsengpa, Lama Jampel Gyatso, Geshe Sherab Drak, Geshe Jampel Tashi, and Geshe Pelkyong.

100 *Milarepa, of days gone by . . .* The great Wensapa (1505-1566) was the learned teacher of Kedrup Sangye Yeshe, who was in turn the teacher of the first Panchen Lama. The "Lobsang Dundrup" of the verse is Wensapa himself, for this was his ordination name. His glowing reference to his own attainments seems presumptuous until we realize that he is referring only to what he hopes he can be, for the verse is found in a section of his writings entitled "Advices to Myself" (see f. 26B, entry 53).

101 *If in your heart . . .* The quoted lines appear on p. 163 of the famous biography of Lord Milarepa by his disciple Rechung Dorje Drakpa (1083–1161); see entry 36.

102 *No way my loved ones know . . .* The lines are found in the section about Lord Milarepa (ff. 72–100) from the *Ocean of Songs of the Kagyu* by Karmapa Mikyu Dorje (1507–1554); see entry 58.

103 *This body of leisure . . .* Another quotation from the very brief version of Lord Tsongkapa's *Steps on the Path to Buddhahood;* see f. 56a, entry 63.

104 *eight ways of lacking opportunity:* These are to hold wrong views, such as believing that what you do does not come back to you; to be born as an animal; birth as an insatiable spirit; birth in the hells; birth in a land where the Buddha's teachings are not available; birth in an "uncivilized" land, where no one keeps the vows of morality; birth as a human who is retarded or otherwise handicapped, so cannot practice the teachings; and birth as a long-lived being of pleasure in one of the temporary paradises (Lord Tsongkapa, pp. 135–7, entry 61; Pabongka Rinpoche, ff. 154b-156b, entry 47; and Master Nagarjuna, pp. 95–6 of the English translation, entry 95).

105 *"Fortune":* The "fortunes" we have are divided into two groups of five: those that relate to ourselves—personal qualities—and those that relate to "others," or the outside world. The first five are to be born as a human; to be born in a "central" land, where people keep the traditional vows of morality; to be born with all one's faculties intact; not to have committed heinous misdeeds, such as killing one's parents; and to have faith in the teachings. The second five are to live in a world where a Buddha has come; where his teachings have been spoken; where the teachings spoken have not been lost; where people still practice them; and where practitioners enjoy the kind support they require (Lord Tsongkapa, entry 61, pp. 137–8; Pabongka Rinpoche, entry 47, ff. 156b-158a).

106 *happier realms:* These consist of the beings who live as humans, as full pleasure beings in the temporary paradises, and as lesser pleasure beings.

107 *benefits that come from keeping your mind on death, etc.:* In his masterwork *Liberation in Our Hands,* Pabongka Rinpoche lists six benefits of keeping your mind on death: your practice becomes really pure; it gains power; the thoughts help you start practice; they help you strive hard during your practice; they help bring your practice to a successful conclusion; and in the hour of death you go with satisfaction, for you know you have spent your life meaningfully.

The Rinpoche also lists six problems that come from not keeping your mind on death: you neglect your religious life, and spend all your days in thoughts of what to eat or wear— this life's distractions; you consider death occasionally but always think it will come later, and delay your practice; or you do practice, but for the wrong reason— with hopes of reputation; you practice but with no enthusiasm, and drop it after a while; you get deeper into this life, your attitude gets worse, and life begins to hurt you; and at death you naturally feel intense regret, for you have wasted all your efforts on this present life.

The three principles, for how actually to keep your mind on death, have three reasons each, making a total of nine. First of all, death is certain: no power in the universe can stop death when it arrives; there is no way to add time to your life, you come closer to death every minute; even while you are alive, the free time available for your practice is extremely limited before you have to die.

The second principle is that there is absolutely no certainty when you will die. We are in a time and realm where the length of life is uncertain; we can be sure we will never have enough time to defeat all our enemies, raise up all our friends, and still complete our religious practice before we die. The things that can kill us are many; the things that keep us alive are few. And in general the body we have is fragile, weak: a small splinter in the hand can give us an infection that kills us—we are like bubbles, like candles in a windstorm.

The third principle is that, at the moment of death, nothing at all can help us but our spiritual practice. None of your money or things can help you. None of your friends or family can help you—they can be holding you tightly by the arms and legs, but still you will slip away alone. And not even your own body can help you—you have to give up your most cherished possession, your beloved body, along with everything else.

The three principles call for three resolves on our part. Knowing that we shall have to die, we must resolve to begin our practice. Knowing that we could die any time, we must quit our worldly work immediately and start our practice today. And finally, since nothing else can help us, we must devote ourselves to our practice only. A man who is hiking many miles doesn't fill up his pack with a lot of crap that he won't be needing.

The above points are paraphrased from the works on the Steps of the path by Lord Tsongkapa (entry 61, ff. 65–75) and Pabongka Rinpoche (entry 47, ff. 168–182). For the last point mentioned in the text, the meditation on what it's like to die, we quote the Rinpoche directly (ff. 182b–183a):

They try all different kinds of treatments and holy rituals but your condition gets worse and worse. The doctors start lying to you. Your friends and relatives say all sorts of cheery things to your face, but behind your back they start wrapping up your affairs, because everyone can see you're going to die.

Your body starts to lose its familiar warmth. It's hard to breathe. The nostrils collapse. The lips curl back. The color starts to drain from your face. All sorts of repulsive signs begin to show, inside and outside of you.

You think of all the wrong things you did in your life, and wish so badly you had never done them. You can't quite be sure if you ever really got rid of them all when you confessed; or that you really did any true good deed.

Then comes the final pain, the unspeakable searing pain that comes with death. The basic building blocks of your body begin their domino collapse, you are blinded by catastrophic images, hallucinations of pure terror crowd into your mind, and carry you away, and the whole world you have been living blinks out.

People take your corpse and wrap it up in a sheet and lay it in some corner. They hang up a curtain to hide it. Somebody lights up a smudgy little candle and leaves it there. If you're one of those reincarnated lamas, they dress you up in your fancy ritual robes and try to make you look good.

Right now we are all running around trying to arrange ourselves a nice house, soft clothes, cozy chairs. But you know the custom here in Tibet—when you die they'll tie your arms and legs up against your chest with a leather strap, carry the body far from town, and throw it naked out on the rocks.

Right now we all go home and try to cook ourselves up some delectable dish—but there will come a day when you stand there praying for a little taste of those cakes they offer the spirits of the dead. Right now we have the big name—they call us Doctor Professor, or Respected Sir, or Your Reverence. But there will come a day when they look at your body and call you nothing but "that stinking corpse." There will come a day when the title they put in front of your name is "the late," or "that guy they used to call . . ."

So now when you respected lamas out there in the audience look at your ritual robes, let it come into your thoughts that these are the robes they will dress your remains in after you have expired. And all the rest of us, when we look at our bedsheets before we go to sleep, should try to remember that these are what they will wrap our stinking corpse in when we die. As Milarepa said,

> That frightful corpse they talk about
> Is the very body you wear, meditator.

He means look at your own body now, and always see the future corpse.

108 *the realms:* See note 14.

109 *Non-virtue brings all sufferings . . .* Quotation from f. 116b of the Master's *Jewel Rosary,* entry 3.

110 *the three rare jewels:* So named because they are supremely valuable and infrequently found—the Buddha, defined as the ultimate shelter, a being who has completed the highest possible good for himself and others; the Dharma, realizations or the end of undesirable qualities within a person's mind; and the Sangha, or any being who has perceived the true nature of reality directly.

111 *the monk named Lekkar:* He spent many years in the service of the Buddha himself but failed miserably to understand his teachings. The dismaying story is found in the twelfth chapter of the *Total-Nirvana Sutra* (ff. 285b-418b, vol. 2, entry 81) and references to it appear often in later literature: see for example f. 136b of Pabongka Rin-

poche's *Liberation* (entry 47); p. 161 of the great Potowa's *Jewels* (entry 19); and f. 5a of the first Panchen Lama's *Path of Bliss* (entry 50)

112 *as well as Devadatta:* A close relation of the Buddha who was driven by jealousy to despise the Teacher. A "heap" of scriptures is sometimes described as the amount you could write with the quantity of ink that Rabten, a fantastic mythical elephant, could carry on his back. One sutra says that Devadatta could recite enough scriptures to make 60,000 loads for the great elephant "Incense." Numerous textual references to the story of the misled monk are listed by Prof. Edgerton (p. 271, entry 92).

113 *an appropriate antidote:* Buddhism teaches that there are four antidote forces, which together can remove the power of any bad deed. The "basis" force consists of thinking who it was that was offended by your deed, and who it is you will rely on to clear yourself of it. The "destruction" force is an intense feeling of shame and regret for the deed, which will certainly return to hurt you. The "reverse" force is to turn yourself away from doing that kind of deed again. The "counteragent" force is to undertake some spiritual practice—confession, meditation, or any good deed—to offset the power of the wrong (see Pabongka Rinpoche, entry 47, ff. 109–113, 246–8).

114 *the ten non-virtues:* The ten non-virtues to be avoided in Buddhist practice are said to be a very gross abbreviation of the many thousands that we do. The ten include three by body (killing any being, stealing, and sexual misconduct); four in speech (lying, divisive speech, harsh words, and idle talk); and three within the mind (coveting others' things, thoughts to harm, and wrong views such as believing that there is no connection between what you do now and what you experience later).

115 *realized being:* Any person who has directly perceived "emptiness"; this will be explained below in the section on correct view.

116 *The path begins* . . . Source of quotation not found.

117 *Revive:* The hell is so named because the inhabitants beat

each other until they all fall down senseless; then they revive and start to fight one another again. The process is repeated over and over for thousands of years, until the beings are finally able to die.

118 *Word of the Gentle One:* Counted among the principal works on the Steps of the path to Buddhahood, and composed by the "Great Fifth" Dalai Lama, Ngawang Lobsang Gyatso (1617-1682); see entry 15. This same Dalai Lama has written two commentaries on the *Three Principal Paths* (entries 16,17).

119 *"Path of Bliss" and "Quick Path":* The former work is another of the classic explanations of the Steps to Buddhahood and was composed by the first of the great Panchen Lamas, Lobsang Chukyi Gyeltsen (1570–1662), who was also the tutor of the above-mentioned Fifth Dalai Lama. The latter treatise was written in explanation of the first by Panchen Lama II, Lobsang Yeshe (see note 97, and entries 50,54).

120 *the fighting:* It is said that the lesser pleasure beings are driven out of attachment and jealousy to wage frequent war on their slightly more glorious cousins, the full pleasure beings.

121 *eight, six, and three types of suffering:* The eight sufferings are being born, getting older, getting sick, dying, encountering things that are unpleasant, losing what is pleasant, trying and failing to get what you want, and the suffering of simply being alive and having all the impure parts of ourselves that we do (Lord Tsongkapa, entry 61, ff. 137-151; Pabongka Rinpoche, entry 47, ff. 250–267). An explanation of the three sufferings follows in the text.

122 *King Mefeed:* A legendary king of yore who was said to have been born spontaneously; he was named from the fact that the concubines of his father competed to breast-feed the miraculous child and thereby become the Queen Mother. His story is mentioned in many works; see Pabongka Rinpoche's *Liberation* (f. 252a), as well as the list in Prof. Edgerton's *Dictionary* under the king's Sanskrit name, Mandhata (p. 430, entry 92).

123 *Keep your wants few* . . . The dictum is expounded upon by the great Buddhist philosopher Vasubandhu (c. 300 A.D.) in the sixth chapter of his classic *Treasure of Wisdom* (see pp. 316-7, entry 14).

124 *If people like these* . . . From the eloquent manual for bodhisattvas by the Buddhist poet-philosopher Shantideva (695-743 A.D.). Quotation on f. 3a, entry 71.

125 *three collections and three trainings:* See note 64.

126 *listeners and self-made victors:* Practicioners who have not yet developed the highest motivation of attaining Buddhahood for the sake of all beings. "Listeners" are so named because they can listen to the higher teachings and relate them to others, but not practice these instructions themselves. "Self-made victors" can reach their goal without relying on a spiritual guide in this life, although only because of extensive instruction by countless teachers in their past lives.

127 *a lower escape:* See note 83.

128 *"enemy destroyers":* Those who have permanently defeated the enemy of mental afflictions—such as desire, anger, and ignorance—and have therefore achieved nirvana. See also note 83.

129 *"The Bodhisattva's Life," "Entering the Middle Way," and "The Rare Stack":* Master Shantideva's manual for bodhisattvas has been listed at note 124. The classic text on correct view by Master Chandrakirti, the illustrious 7th Century Indian philosopher of Buddhism, will be covered below with the third of the principal paths. In each case, the benefits of the wish for enlightenment appear in the opening verses. *The Rare Stack* is a separate section of the Buddhist canon containing some 49 different sutras. One often quoted in explanations of the wish for Buddhahood is *The Chapter of Light Protector* (entry 75); it contains eloquent descriptions of the benefits of the wish throughout, and the section around f. 237 is particularly relevant here.

130 *Even just wishing* . . . Quotation on f. 3a of this textbook for bodhisattvas (entry 71).

131 *Were the merit of the wish . . .* Quotation from f. 352b of this teaching of the Buddha himself (entry 11).

132 *Loving-Gaze:* The divine form of the Buddha that represents all his compassion. The practice mentioned can be learned from a qualified lama.

133 *Commentary on Valid Perception:* Famed treatise which forms the basis for the study of formal logic in Buddhist monasteries. It was composed by Master Dharmakirti (c. 630 A.D.) in explanation of the *Compendium on Valid Perception* written by Master Dignaga (c. 450 A.D.), great forefather of the Buddhist logic traditions. The reasoning mentioned is found in the second chapter, the "Proof of Infallibility," beginning from line 142 (ff. 108b-109a, entry 22).

134 *preventing a person from slipping:* Some discussions of these benefits appear in Lord Tsongkapa's work on ff. 182-6 and 189 (entry 61).

135 *"beautiful" form of loving-kindness:* Means to see every other living creature as beautiful or beloved as one's only child; this loving-kindness is distinguished from the one mentioned next.

136 *twenty-two forms of the wish:* These metaphors are found on f. 2b of the *Jewel of Realizations* (see note 69). Here the wish for enlightenment is compared to earth, gold, the first day's moon, fire, a mine, a cache of gemstones, the ocean, a diamond, the king of mountains, medicine, a spiritual guide, a wish-giving jewel, the sun, a song, a king, a treasure, a highway, a riding horse, a fountain of water, a sweet sound, a river, and a cloud. Each metaphor stands for the wish at a different level of realization; the venerable Lama of Chone, Drakpa Shedrup (1675-1748) gives a concise explanation of them in his commentary (pp. 45-6, entry 13).

The distinction between "praying" for and "engaging" in the wish for enlightenment is described as the difference between wanting to go somewhere and then actually stepping along with the resolve to reach the goal. In the latter case one has taken the formal vows for the wish and is acting with the conscious intention of attaining enlightenment for all living beings. See pp. 109–110 of entry 31, the commentary to the *Jewel* by Kedrup Tenpa Dargye (1493–1568), a renowned scholar from Pabongka Rinpoche's own Sera Mey College.

137 *Many eons the Able Lords . . .* This quotation found on f. 2a; the preceding reference is on f. 7b (entry 71).

138 *Center beam of the highest way . . .* Again from the very brief version of his *Steps on the Path* (p. 310, entry 63). The entire context reads as follows:

> Center beam of the highest way, the wish;
> Foundation, support for those of mighty deeds;
> Alchemist elixir for turning both the collections;
> Gold mine of merit, full of a mass of good.
> Bodhisattva princes, knowing this,
> Keep the high jewel wish their center practice.

The "two collections" are the accumulations of knowledge and virtue which produce the bodies of a Buddha (see note 32).

139 *the Elimination Ritual, etc.:* We have not located the spurious texts listed.

140 *Three Heaps Sutra, etc.:* These four teachings of the Buddha himself are listed at entries 39, 21, 33, and 10 respectively.

141 *Buddha-Dharma-Sangha prayer:* A traditional prayer for refuge and developing the wish for enlightenment. It reads,

> I go for refuge, until I reach enlightenment,
> To the Buddha, Dharma, and the highest Sangha.
> By the merit of giving and other goods deeds I do
> May I become a Buddha to help all living beings.

The Buddha, Dharma, and Sangha are explained in note 110.

142 *Stages of Meditation:* The point is discussed by Lord Tsongkapa at ff. 89–92 of his shorter *Steps on the Path* (entry 60), and ff. 191–202 in his longer version (entry 61). Here a number of times he quotes the *Stages of Meditation*, a treatise in three parts by the eighth-century Bud-

dhist master Kamalashila (entry 1). Kamalashila is best known for his successful defense of the Indian Buddhist teaching of analytical meditation before the Tibetan king Trisong Detsen. His opponents were Chinese monks who wrongly asserted that meditating on nothing at all would be of any benefit.

143 *path of preparation:* Another set of five paths, or levels of realization, is described in Buddhism. Included are the paths of accumulation, preparation, seeing, habituation, and "no more learning." The five for the "greater" way differ from those of the "lesser" way (see note 56).

144 *all eight levels:* Refers to intensely deep forms of meditation that lead to later births in the eight sections of the form and formless realms, which are still counted as suffering (see note 14).

145 *The worldly meditate on concentration* . . . The verse is found on ff. 44a-44b of this famous teaching of the Buddha (see entry 23). The following citation is the next verse in the sutra, from f. 44b. The wording of the edition available to us is slightly different, but the intent equal. Udraka was a non-Buddhist sage who woke from an extended period of meditation and went into a rage because mice had in the meantime chewed away at his impressive yogi's locks of hair; because of his anger, he was then born in the hells.

146 *There is no second door* . . . Quotation from f. 13b of Master Aryadeva's work (see entry 40 and note 79).

147 *Wisdom not steeped in method* . . . The lines appear on f. 313a of this well-known sutra, and are clarified by it immediately afterward (see entry 35).

148 *By this virtue may all beings* . . . Final lines of the Master's *Sixty Verses of Reasoning,* and often used nowadays as a prayer of dedication after the good deed of listening to a teaching. Original from f. 22b, entry 5.

149 *On vast wide-spreading wings* . . . Quotation on f. 212a of *Entering the Middle Way* (see entry 74 and note 129).

150 *Understanding that Has No End:* A famed teaching of the Buddha requested by a disciple of this name (entry 49).

The *Root Wisdom* of Master Nagarjuna (c. 200 A.D.) is listed at entry 4; for other works of his famed "Collection," see the biography in the English translation of his *Letter to a Friend* (p. 10, entry 95).

151 *the masters Buddhapalita, etc.:* For the commentary of Master Buddhapalita (c. 500 A.D.), see entry 85. Master Aryadeva's work has already been listed (see note 79), as has Master Chandrakirti's *Entering the Middle Way* (note 129). For *A Clarification of the Words,* see entry 73.

152 *There's no way to peace . . .* From the sixth chapter of Master Chandrakirti's work (f. 205a, entry 74). Briefly, the "two truths" mentioned are what are usually called "deceptive truth" and "ultimate truth." Both are valid, and all objects have both. The dependence of objects (especially in the sense described below, upon concepts and names) is their conventional or deceptive truth. Their appearance is "deceptive" because to the minds of normal people they appear to be something other than what they actually are. The "ultimate" (here called "real") truth of objects is their lack of non-dependence, and is first seen directly in the all-important meditative state known as the "path of seeing." Seeing this truth directly acts immediately to stop the process through which we suffer.

153 *Nagarjuna's student was Chandrakirti . . .* The lines are from his work on the two truths; see f. 72a, entry 56.

154 *"Detailist" school:* So called because "they devote their study exclusively to the classical commentary known as *Detailed Exposition,* or else because they understand the *Exposition*'s meaning" (the First Dalai Lama, entry 14, p. 14).

155 *"Scripturalist" school:* The name is said to come from the fact that "this school of philosophers holds that scripture [eg. sutra] is valid, but denies the validity of classical commentaries such as the Seven Works on Knowledge" (ibid).

156 *"Mind-Only" school:* The name comes from the school's assertion that "every existing object is nothing but part of the mind," although this general description is further refined by the school.

157 *made from any different "substance":* That is, come from any different principal cause or latency.

158 *"Independent" part of the Middle Way school:* The school is so named because its followers advocate a middle way which avoids the extreme of thinking things exist (naturally) and the extreme of thinking things can't exist (if they don't exist naturally). The "Independents" are one of the two parts of the school; they believe one must lead a person to the correct view that things are empty of natural existence by means of taking an independent object and discussing it in common terms—rather than starting from the person's own incorrect view and demonstrating the absurdity that it necessarily implies. These points are illuminated by the great Changkya Rolpay Dorje, said to be a former life of Pabongka Rinpoche himself, in his *Comparative Systems* (pp. 289, 305, 325; entry 80).

159 *unaffected awareness:* Any normal, "reasonable" perception—the vast majority of our everyday perceptions; the opposite would be those infrequent cases where we take something wrong, such as mistaking a moving leaf for a small animal as we drive a car, or believing in something unreal that we think we see under the influence of alcohol or a drug.

160 *"Implication" section of the Middle Way school:* So named because of their belief that a line of reasoning which implies a necessary absurdity in an opponent's incorrect view on the subject is sufficient to inspire in his mind the correct view of the nature of existence (again see Changkya Rolpay Dorje, p. 407, entry 80).

161 *"Functionalist" group:* Refers collectively to the Detailist, Scripturalist, and Mind-Only schools, since all assert that functional things exist truly.

162 *the fourfold analysis:* Briefly, Pabongka Rinpoche lists the four as follows in his treatise on the Steps (entry 47, ff. 362–377):

> 1) *Identify what you deny:* any object that could exist truly. You cannot catch a thief if you don't know what he looks like.

2) *Recognize the necessity:* that if an object exists truly, it must be truly one or truly many.

3) *Perceive that it is not truly one:* if you were truly your parts, you couldn't say "parts," since you are only one.

4) *Perceive that it is not truly many:* if your parts were truly you, then when you took any one part it would be you—the same way you get a cow when you have a goat and a sheep and a cow and take out the goat and the sheep.

The conclusion is that since you are neither truly one nor truly many, you do not truly exist. Lord Tsongkapa discusses these points on ff. 374–475 of his greater Steps (entry 61).

163 *destructible view:* This way of looking at things is called "destructible" both because it focuses on me, and I will one day perish, and because the wrong view itself will one day be corrected and disappear.

164 *Here what we call a self . . .* Quotation from his commentary on the *400 Verses* of Master Aryadeva (note 79). See f. 187b, entry 72.

165 *Since every object is labelled . . .* Found on p. 396 of entry 45.

166 *Like an illusion . . .* The full line is found of f. 16a of the work, entry 70.

167 *Once you grasp the secret . . .* Source of quotation not found.

168 *precious teacher Chone Lama:* Refers to Pabongka Rinpoche's teacher named Chone Geshe Lobsang Gyatso Trin.

169 *Therefore this proof employing interdependence . . .* Quotation from his *Entering the Middle Way,* ff. 206b-207a (entry 74).

170 *Everything is right . . .* Quotation from f. 15a of Master Nagarjuna's masterpiece (entry 4).

171 *Form is emptiness* . . . From the famous *Heart of Wisdom Sutra*, f. 259b (entry 20).

172 *eight worldly thoughts:* They were listed above in section VIII, on "Stopping Desire for This Life."

173 *three "countless" eons:* The word "countless" here actually refers to a specific number—1,000,000,000,000,000, 000,000,000,000,000,000,000,000,000,000,000,000,000. The length of an "eon" is variously described in Buddhist scripture, and is tied to cycles in the lifespans of beings; suffice to say it entails millions of years.

174 *Steps of the path!* Original source of quotation not found. Pabongka Rinpoche's *Liberation* twice credits the three instructions to Gompa Rinchen Lama (entry 47, ff. 168a, 334a), who is said to have been a student of Lord Atisha (see Lord Tsongkapa's *Greater Steps,* entry 61, f. 12a), and of Lord Drom Tonpa (*Blue Annals,* entry 94, p. 264). Geshe Dolpa, full name Marshurpa Rok Sherab Gyatso (1059–1131) was a student of the great Potowa and compiled his mentor's teachings into a famed text of the Seer tradition entitled the *Blue Book* (see its commentary at entry 89).

175 *Don't be a quitter* . . . From the chapter on effort in Master Shantideva's classic (f. 20a, entry 71). "Those who've Gone That Way" refers to the Buddhas.

176 *the glorious Lobsang Drakpa:* As mentioned in the Foreword, this was Lord Tsongkapa's ordination name.

177 *the proper series of visualizations:* The section that follows was included in Pabongka Rinpoche's commentary for the benefit of his disciples already familiar with the practice. It is translated here for completeness, but like any Buddhist teaching requires the personal guidance of a qualified lama for successful results.

178 *Collection Field:* Traditional paintings of this visualization are fairly common; one good example appears in the Newark Museum's catalogue (illustration P20, p. 170, entry 93). The name of the visualization is meant to show that these holy beings are the best field in which one can plant the seeds of his enlightenment: the two collections of

merit and wisdom. The symbolism of the picture is detailed carefully by Pabongka Rinpoche in his *Liberation in Our Hands* (ff. 92–102, entry 47).

179 *"Path of Bliss" or "Quick Path":* See note 119.

180 *attitudes as these people have them:* As mentioned above (note 20), the practitioner of lesser scope seeks to save himself from the lower realms. The practitioner of medium scope hopes to escape from all forms of suffering life, even the higher realms. The practitioner of the greatest scope shares these attitudes, but seeks equally to assure that every other being reaches these goals too.

181 *huge black sow:* Also stands for ignorance, the root of all our suffering.

182 *two reasons for taking refuge:* These are (1) to fear the lower realms and cyclic life in general, and (2) to believe that the three jewels have the power to protect you (see note 110).

183 *the "immeasurables":* These are immeasurable loving-kindness, compassion, joy, and neutrality; they are described in a classic verse, respectively, as follows:

> May all living beings gain happiness and
>   what causes happiness.
> May all living beings escape suffering and
>   what causes suffering.
> May all living beings never be without the
>   happiness free of every suffering.
> May all living beings stay neutral, free of
>   all like for their friends and dislike
>   for their enemies.

The four are called "immeasurable" because they are thoughts directed at an immeasurable number of beings, and because one gains immeasurable merit from thinking them. There is another set of four attitudes with the same names, known collectively as the "four places of the Pure One." Pabongka Rinpoche elsewhere explains that the loving-kindness of this set covers many, but not all, sentient beings, and so one who meditates upon it is born as a being like the worldly god named Pure One, whose authority extends over many, but not all, places. By focussing on all beings, one achieves nirvana "without a place" (beyond both this suffering world and a lower nirvana) as the Great Pure One (another name for a full Buddha) (see ff. 308b-309a, entry 47).

184 *special wish for Buddhahood:* The lines read "For the sake of all my mother beings, I will do anything I have to in order to reach precious total enlightenment, as fast as I can. Thus I will now begin a meditation on the teaching of the Steps on the path to Buddhahood, using the profound path of practice that centers upon my lama, my god" (f. 5a, entry 26).

185 *Eight Thousand Verses:* One of the most famed and eloquent sutras on the perfection of wisdom, or correct view (entry 83).

186 *the Great Tutor, the Holder of the Diamond:* Probably refers to Pabongka Rinpoche's root master, Dakpo Lama Jampel Hlundrup.

187 *"Knowledge Unlocks the World":* See note 40 on these lines composed by Lord Tsongkapa himself.

188 *"Offering to Lamas" manual:* See note 43; the Great Seal is a practice of the secret teachings.

189 *"Unsurpassed" group, etc.:* These refer to the four traditional classes of the secret teachings.

190 *"Secret Collection," etc.:* The beings mentioned are all forms which the Buddha takes to give the secret teachings, and belong to the "Unsurpassed" group.

191 *body mandala in the "Offering to Lamas":* See pp. 44-7 of the work (entry 51).

192 *May this good deed* . . . Final verses of "Knowledge Unlocks the World" (pp. 207-8, entry 65). They read as follows:

> May this good deed, standing for whatever
> ones are done
> By myself and others throughout all
> of the three times
> Never even for a single moment

in the many
Lives we take give forth its fruit
by turning into something
Which will lead us to the kinds of things
the world hopes for:
Gains that put themselves ahead, or else
some reputation,
Crowds of followers, life's enjoyments,
others' gifts and honors;
Rather may it only bring us enlightenment
unmatched.
By the wondrous blessings of the Victors
and their sons,
By the truth that interdependence
cannot ever fail,
By the might of my willingness to free
all beings myself,
May all that I have prayed for here
so purely come to pass.

193 *same with the savior Serlingpa:* Again refers to Pabongka
Rinpoche's root teacher, Dakpo Lama Rinpoche (see note
186). Lama Serlingpa, also known as Dharmakirti (but
different from the sage of the same name who composed
the *Commentary on Valid Perception*), was a great master
of the teachings on the wish for enlightenment. He lived
in what is now Indonesia and instructed Lord Atisha for
twelve years (see note 49).

194 *to the good of every living being:* Among the verses that
Pabongka Rinpoche spoke in his final prayer of dedication
was the following. It comes from the end of *The Hundred
Gods of Bliss Paradise* (see entry 86), which is a lama-
practice text centered on the great Tsongkapa, Lobsang
Drakpa:

May whatever virtue I've collected in
this deed of mine
Be of all possible benefit to all beings
and the teachings.
Especially may it help me to illuminate
for long

193

The inner essence of the teachings
Lobsang Drakpa gave.

195 *deep thought of the Victors:* "Victors" refers to the Buddhas; in our world, the instructions of the Steps of the path to Buddhahood have been passed down along two great lineages: the Steps on correct view through disciples of Master Nagarjuna, who learned them from the divine being Gentle Voice; and the Steps on the wish for enlightenment through disciples of Master Asanga, who heard them from Loving One—the Future Buddha.

It is a tradition of Tibetan poetics to weave a great personage's name into a verse, often with special marks under the appropriate syllables. Here the italics stand for Pabongka Rinpoche's full name (see the Foreword).

196 *spewed out from his lips:* Poetic metaphor based on a traditional belief that the mongoose vomits up jewels. The "ten forces" are the ten supreme forms of knowledge possessed by a Buddha, such as knowing perfectly what is actual and what is not, and exactly how deeds will ripen upon a person. The words "shining fame" are a pun on the second part of Lord Tsongkapa's ordination name, Lobsang Drakpa, since *drakpa* means "famed."

197 *their son, a child:* Lord Tsongkapa is said to have actually been a Buddha who appeared to his disciples in the form of a bodhisattva, or a "son of the Victors." The word "child" is an allusion to the youthful aspect in which Gentle Voice sometimes appears.

198 *eighty thousand:* Refers to the 84,000 different masses of teaching or "heaps of scripture" imparted by the Buddhas (see note 112).

199 *world or peace, wherever:* Refers in this case to the world and what transcends it.

200 *both the bodies:* See note 32. The mental body is caused primarily by correct view; the physical body by activities motivated by the wish for enlightenment. See also text related to note 148.

201 *three kinds of kindness:* In the tradition of the open teachings, a lama pays his student the kindnesses of granting

him personal instructions, oral transmissions, and formal explanations of scripture. Within the secret tradition, he allows the student initiation, explanation, and advices.

202 *Suddhi Vadzra:* Tibetan transliteration for the Sanskrit equivalent of the name of the Tibetan editor, Lobsang Dorje. His home district was Den Ma, in the southeast of Tibet (see also Foreword).

203 *Tashi Chuling:* Pabongka Rinpoche's mountain hermitage; see Foreword.

204 *Gungtang:* Refers to Gungtang Jampeyang; see note 62. This "Key" to the *Three Principal Paths* is found in his collected works (see entry 9) and is followed by an instruction (entry 8) on how to perform a formal meditation session upon the three paths, using the lines of Lord Tsongkapa's original text.

205 *six preliminaries:* The six practices before a meditation session are cleaning one's room and setting up an altar, putting forth offerings, sitting in the proper posture and preparing one's mind by the thoughts of seeking refuge and the wish for enlightenment, visualizing the traditional assemblage of holy beings, going through the steps of gathering virtue and removing bad deeds, and then supplicating the lamas. See also note 177.

206 *a kind of even-mindedness:* The phrase itself is a double entendre, since the second system's first step is neutrality towards all beings (see section XII, "How to Develop the Wish for Enlightenment").

207 *"think of what's happening":* This phrase as well is lifted from the eighth verse of Lord Tsongkapa's root text, and then played upon.

208 *Tashi:* A common Tibetan personal name.

209 *far from correct view yourself:* The tenets of the lower Buddhist schools concerning "no-self" have been explained above in section XIV, "Why You Need Correct View."

210 *the so-called "Cast-Offs":* A philosophical school of ancient India, considered one of the crudest since they did

not accept the concepts of past and future lives, and the relation between one's past deeds and present experiences.

211 *the house of Hlalu:* A well-known aristocratic family of old Tibet. Their principal holdings were located to the north-west of Lhasa, on the road to Drepung Monastery.

BIBLIOGRAPHY

We would like to acknowledge the assistance of Robert Lacey, Artemus Engle, and Susan Meinheit in compiling the bibliography and notes. Information on many of the works and authors mentioned is as yet far from standardized; dates are taken for the most part from Roerich, Vostrikov, and available Library of Congress listings. These last are a tremendous resource resulting from the selfless efforts of E. Gene Smith over the entire length of the Library's commendable SFCP foreign texts collection program.

Some of the works listed below include both Tibetan and Western pagination; these are indicated by "f" (folio) and "p" (page) respectively. The following abbreviations are also used:

KG = *bKa'-'gyur* collection of Buddhist scripture, in 101 vols. Lhasa: Zhol par-khang, 1934; microfiche edition Stony Brook, New York: Institute for Advanced Studies of World Religions, 1974.

TG = *bsTan-'gyur* collection of Buddhist commentary, in 209 vols. Co-ne, Tibet: Co-ne dgon chen, c. 1725; microfiche edition also available from IASWR.

Toh = UI, PROF. HAKUJU, et al. *A Complete Catalogue of the Tibetan Buddhist Canons (Bkaḥ-ḥgyur and Bstan-ḥgyur),* in 2 vols. Sendai, Japan: Tohoku Imperial University, 1934 (for ref. nos. 1-4569).
    KANAKURA, PROF. YENSHO, et al. *Catalogue of the Tohoku University Collection of Tibetan*

Works on Buddhism. Sendai, Japan: The Seminary of Indology, Tohoku University, 1953 (for ref. nos. 5001-7083).

A. Works in Tibetan and Sanskrit

1 (SLOB-DPON) KA-MA-LA-SH'I-LA (KAMALAŚĪLA). *bsGom-pa'i-rim-pa (Bhāvanākrama)*, ff. 22a-42b (first); 42b-56b (second); 56b-70a (third); vol. 31 (ki) in the dBu-ma section of the TG. Toh refs. 3915, 3916, 3917.

2 (SA-SKYA PANDI-TA) KUN-DGA' RGYAL-MTSAN. *sDom-pa gsum-gyi rab-tu dbye-ba'i bstan-bcos bzhugs-so*. sGang-tog: n.p., 1967?, 101 ff.

3 (DPAL-MGON 'PHAGS-PA) KLU-SGRUB (NĀGĀRJUNA). *rGyal-po la gtam-bya-ba rin-po-che'i phreng-ba (Rājāparikathāratna-mālā)*, ff. 116a-135a, vol. 93 (ge) in the sPring-yig section of the TG. Toh ref. 4158.

4 _____ . *dBu-ma rtza-ba'i tsig-le'ur byas-pa shes-rab ces-bya-ba (rTza-ba shes-rab) (Prajñānāmamūlamadhyamaka-kārikā)*, ff. 1a-19a, vol. 17 (tza) in the dBu-ma section of the TG. Toh ref. 3824.

5 _____ . *Rigs-pa drug-cu-pa'i tsig-le'ur byas-pa zhes-bya-ba (Yuktiṣaṣṭikākārikānāma)*, ff. 20a-22b, vol. 17 (tza) in the dBu-ma section of the TG. Toh ref. 3825.

6 _____ . *bShes-pa'i spring-yig (Suhṛllekha)*, ff. 40b-46a, vol. 94 (nge) in the sPring-yig section of the TG. Toh ref. 4182.

7 (DBAL-MANG) DKON-MCHOG RGYAL-MTSAN. *Lam-gyi gtzo-bo rnam gsum gyi zin-tho*, pp. 531-552, vol. 5 of collected works. New Delhi: Gyaltan Gelek Namgyal, 1974, 629 pp.

8 (GUNG-THANG 'JAM-PA'I DBYANGS) DKON-MCHOG BSTAN-PA'I SGRON-ME. *Lam gyi gtzo-bo rnam-gsum rtza-tsig gi steng nas gzhungs-bsrangs te, nyams-su len-tsul*, pp. 641-49 in vol. 3 (ga) of collected works. New Delhi: Gedan Sungrab Minyam Gyunphel Series, Ngawang Gelek Demo, 1972, 934 pp.

9 _____ . *Lam-gtzo'i zin-bris gsang-ba'i lde-mig*, pp. 639-40 appended to *Byang-chub kyi sems gnyis sgom-tsul theg-pa*

mchog gi 'jug-ngogs zhes-bya-ba bzhugs-so, pp. 621-40 in vol. 3 (ga) of collected works (ibid).

10 *('Phags-pa) bsKal-pa bzang-po zhes-bya-ba theg-pa chen-po'i mdo (mDo-sde bskal-bzang) (Āryabhadrakalpika-nāmamahāyānasūtra),* ff. 1b-548a, vol. 1 (ka) in the mDo-mang section of the KG. Toh ref. 94.

11 *('Phags-pa) Khyim-bdag dPas-byin gyis zhus-pa zhes-bya-ba theg-pa chen-po'i mdo* (variant spellings *dPa'* and *dPal*) *(Āryavīradattagṛhapatiparipṛcchānāmamahāyānasūtra),* ff. 339a-355a, vol. 5 (ca) in the dKon-brtzegs section of the KG, etc. Tohoku ref. 72.

12 (RJE-BTZUN) GRAGS-PA RGYAL-MTSAN. *Zhen-pa bzhi-bral bzhugs-so,* pp. 436-39 of the collection *Sems-dpa' chen-po dKon-mchog rgyal-mtsan gyis phyogs-bsgrigs mdzad-pa'i blo-sbyong brgya-rtza dang dkar-chag gdung-sel zla-ba bcas bzhugs-so.* Dharamsala, India: Shes-rig par-khang, 1973, 478 pp. Several related texts follow in the collection.

13 (CO-NE RJE-BTZUN) GRAGS-PA BSHAD-SGRUB. *rGyan gyi ṭi-ka zhes-bya-ba bzhugs-so.* Bylakuppe, India: Sermey Monastery Printing Press, 1988, 233 pp.

14 (RGYAL-BA) DGE-'DUN GRUB-PA. *Dam-pa'i chos mngon-pa mdzod kyi rnam-par bshad-pa thar-lam gsal-byed ces-bya-ba.* Varanasi, India: W'a-ṇa mtho-slob dge-ldan spyi-las khang, 1973, 391 pp. Toh ref. 5525.

15 (RGYAL-MCHOG LNGA-PA) NGAG-DBANG BLO-BZANG RGYA-MTSO. *Byang-chub lam gyi rim-pa'i 'khrid-yig 'Jam-pa'i dbyangs kyi zhal-lung zhes-bya-ba bzhugs-so.* Thim-bu: Kun-bzang stobs-rgyal, 1976, 108 ff. Toh ref. 5637.

16 _____ . *Lam gyi gtzo-bo rnam gsum gyi mchan-'grel,* 4 ff. in vol. 12 (na) of collected works, edition held at the Beinecke Rare Book and Manuscript Library, Yale University Library, New Haven. Toh ref. 5641.

17 _____ . *Lam gtzo rnam gsum gyi dgongs-'grel lung-rigs gter-mdzod,* 26 ff. in vol. 12 (na) of collected works (ibid).

LCANG-SKYA ROL-PA'I RDO-RJE: see (lCang-skya rol-pa'i rdo-rje) Ye-shes bstan-pa'i sgron-me.

18 (bTzun-pa) LCE-SGOM. *bKa'-gdams kyi skyes-bu dam-pa rnams kyi gsung-bgros thor-bu-ba rnams bzhugs-so*, ff 1b-51a of 60. N.p., n.d.: modern Indian reprint sponsored by dGe-slong Thub-bstan don-yod with a printing prayer by sKyabs-rje Khri-byang rin-po-che. Note: There is some confusion about the author's dates and exact name; we have listed as reported in this and the following text. We see the variant *sPyil-sgom rdzong-pa Shes-rab rdo-rje* in the *bKa'-gdams chos-'byung* of Paṇ-chen bSod-nams grags-pa; there is also a *lCe-btzun Seng-ge dbang-phyug* pictured in the *Iconography* of Lokesh Chandra (figure #1722, see entry 90 below).

19 LCE-SGOM-PA (SHES-RAB RDO-RJE). *dPe-chos rin-chen spungs-pa'i 'bum-'grel*. Sarnath, Varanasi: The Pleasure [*sic*] of Elegant Sayings Printing Press, 1965, 366 pp.

20 *bCom-ldan-'das-ma shes-rab kyi pha-rol-tu phyin-pa'i snying-po (Shes-rab snying-po) (Bhagavatīprajñāpāram-itāhṛdaya)*, ff. 259a-261a, vol. 1 (ka) in the Sher-phyin sna-tsogs section of the KG. Toh ref. 21 (also found at 531).

21 ('Phags-pa) *bCom-ldan-'das sman gyi bla bai-ḍ'urya'i 'od-kyi sngon gyi lam gyi khyad-par rgyas-pa zhes-bya-ba theg-pa chen-po'i mdo (sMan bla'i mdo) (Āryabhagavatobhaiṣ-ajyaguruvaiḍūryaprabhāsyapūrvapraṇidhānaviśeṣavi-stāranāmamahāyānasūtra)*, ff. 419a-433b, vol. 9 (ta) in the rGyud section of the KG. Toh ref. 504.

22 (SLOB-DPON) CHOS-KYI GRAGS-PA (DHARMAKĪRTI). *Tsad-ma rnam-'grel gyi tsig-le'ur byas-pa (Pramāṇavarttikakārikā)*, ff. 94a-151b, vol. 95 (ce) in the Tsad-ma section of the TG. Toh ref. 4210.

23 ('Phags-pa) *Chos thams-cad kyi rang-bzhin mnyam-pa nyid rnam-par spros-pa ting-nge-'dzin gyi rgyal-po zhes-bya-ba theg-pa chen-po'i mdo (mDo ting-nge-'dzin gyi rgyal-po) (Āryasarvadharmasvabhāvasamatāvipañcitasamādhi-rājanāmamahāyānasūtra)*, ff. 1b-269b, vol. 9 (ta) in the mDo-mang section of the KG. Toh ref. 127.

24 *mChog gi dang-po'i sangs-rgyas las byung-ba rgyud kyi rgyal-po dpal dus kyi 'khor-lo zhes-bya-ba (Paramādibud-*

dhoddhṛtaśrīkālacakranāmatantrarājā), ff. 28b-186b, vol. 1 (ka) in the rGyud-'bum section of the KG. Toh ref. 362.

25 *('Phags-pa) 'Jam-dpal ye-shes sems-dpa'i don-dam-pa'i mtsan yang-dag-par brjod-pa ('Jam-dpal mtsan-brjod) (Mañjuśrījñānasattvasyaparamārthanāmasaṃgīti)*, ff. 1b-19a, vol. 1 (ka) of the rGyud-'bum section of the KG. Toh ref. 360.

26 (DVAGS-PO BLA-MA RIN-PO-CHE) 'JAM-DPAL LHUN-GRUB. *Byang-chub lam gyi rim-pa'i dmar-khrid myur-lam gyi sngon-'gro'i 'don gyi rim-pa khyer-bde bklags-chog bskal-bzang mgrin-rgyan zhes-bya-ba bzhugs-so.* Kalimpong, India: Mani Printing Works, c. 1965, 25 ff.

27 (KUN-MKHYEN) 'JAM-DBYANGS BSHAD-PA'I RDO-RJE. *Rje-btzun Tzong-kha-pa chen-po'i rnam-thar ras-bris kyi tsul brgya nga-gsum-pa tzinta-ma-ṇi'i phreng-ba thub-bstan rgyas-byed phan-bde'i rol-mtso chen-po*, pp. 285-336 of vol. 4 (nga) of collected works. New Delhi: Ngawang Gelek Demo, 1972.

28 *('Phags-pa) sNying-rje padma dkar-po zhes-bya-ba theg-pa chen-po'i mdo (sNying-rje pad-dkar) (Āryakāruṇāpuṇḍarīkanāmamahāyānasūtra)*, ff. 209b-474a of vol. 6 (cha) in the mDo-mang section of the KG, etc. Toh ref. 112.

29 (SLOB-DPON) RTA-DBYANGS (AŚVAGHOṢA). *Bla-ma lnga-bcu-pa (Gurupañcāśikā)*, ff. 9b-11b, vol. 207 (tsu) in the rGyud section of the TG. Toh ref. 3721.

30 BSTAN-DAR LHA-RAMS-PA. *Lam gyi gtzo-bo gsum gyi 'grel-pa 'dod-'jo'i dpag-bsam zhes-bya-ba bzhugs-so*, pp. 323-370, vol. 1 (ka) of collected works. New Delhi: Lama Guru Deva, 1971, 755 pp.

31 (MKHAS-GRUB) BSTAN-PA DAR-RGYAS (DPAL BZANG-PO). *bsTan-bcos mngon-par rtog-pa'i rgyan rtza-'grel gyi spyi-don rnam-bshad snying-po rgyan gyi snang-ba zhes-bya-ba bzhugs-so (Phar-phyin spyi-don).* New Delhi: printing sponsored by Geshe Lobsang Tharchin, 1980, 604 pp.

32 (A-CHI THU-NO-MON-HAN BLO-BZANG YE-SHES) BSTAN-PA RAB-RGYAS. *Collected Works.* Dharamṣala, India: Library of Tibetan Works and Archives, 1985. Toh refs. 6199-6257.

33 (*'Phags-pa) Thar-pa chen-po phyogs-su rgyas-pa 'gyod-tsangs kyis sdig sbyangs te sangs-rgyas su grub-par rnam-par bkod-pa zhes-bya-ba theg-pa chen-po'i mdo (Thar-pa chen-po'i mdo) (Āryamahāmokṣadiśunpuṣyakrokramtyapāpamśodhananāmaviharatisma)*, ff. 423a-506a, vol. 21 (zha) of the mDo-mang section of the KG. Toh ref. 264.

34 (SLOB-DPON) DAṆḌI (DBYUG-PA-CAN) (DAṆḌIN). *sNyan-ngag me-long (Kāvyādarśa)*, ff. 322a-345b, vol. 118 (se) in the sGra-mdo section of the TG. Toh ref. 4301.

35 (*'Phags-pa) Dri-ma med-par grags-pas bstan-pa zhes-bya-ba theg-pa chen-po'i mdo (Āryavimalakīrtinirdeśanāma-mahāyānasūtra)*, ff. 270b-376b, vol. 14 (pha) in the mDo-mang section of the KG. Toh ref. 176.

36 (RAS-CHUNG) RDO-RJE GRAGS-PA. *rNal-'byor gyi dbang-phyug dam-pa rje-btzun Mi-la-ras-pa'i rnam-thar thar-pa dang thams-cad mkhyen-pa'i lam-ston bzhugs-so.* Modern edition from blocks stored at the monastery of Chitari in Kulu Manali, India, 639 pp.

37 (DNGUL-CHU) DHARMA BHADRA. *Lam gyi gtzo-bo rnam gsum gyi ṭ'i-ka tsig-don rab-tu gsal-bar byed-pa'i sgron-me*, pp. 487-511 in vol. 5 of collected works. New Delhi: Champa Oser, 1973, 445 pp. Toh ref. 6404.

38 ———— . *Lam gyi gtzo-bo gsum gyi 'khrid-yig skal-ldan 'jug-ngogs sogs*, pp. 133-145 in vol. 3 of collected works (ibid), 799 pp. Toh ref. 6342.

PHA-BONG-KHA-PA: see (sKyabs-rje Pha-bong-kha-pa rje-btzun) Byams-pa bstan-'dzin 'phrin-las rgya-mtso (dpal bzang-po).

39 (*'Phags-pa) Phung-po gsum-pa zhes-bya-ba theg-pa chen-po'i mdo (Phung-po gsum-pa'i mdo) (Āryatriskandhaka-nāmamahāyānasūtra)*, ff. 133b-164a, vol. 22 (za) of the mDo-mang section of the KG. Toh ref. 284.

40 (SLOB-DPON) 'PHAGS-PA LHA (ĀRYADEVA). *bsTan-bcos bzhi-brgya-pa zhes-bya-ba'i tsig-le'ur byas-pa (bZhi-brgya-pa) (Catuḥśatakaśāstrakārikānāma)*, ff. 1a-18a, vol. 18 (tsa) in the dBu-ma section of the TG. Toh ref. 3846.

41 (RGYAL-DBANG) 'PHRIN-LAS RNAM-RGYAL. *'Jam-mgon chos*

kyi rgyal-po Tzong-kha-pa chen-po'i rnam-thar thub-bstan mdzes-pa'i rgyan gcig ngo-mtsar nor-bu'i 'phreng-ba (rNam-thar chen-mo). Sarnath, India: Sa-ra-ṇa-tha'i legs-bshad gter-mdzod khang, 1967, 636 pp.

42 *Bod-rgya tsig-mdzod chen-mo,* 3 vols. Beijing: Mi-rigs dpe-skrun khang, 1985.

43 (RJE-BTZUN) BYAMS-PA (MAITREYA). *Theg-pa chen-po'i mdo-sde'i rgyan zhes-bya-ba'i tsig-le'ur byas-pa (Mahāyānasūtrā-laṃkāranāmakārikā),* ff. 1a-37a, vol. 44 (phi) in the Sems-tzam section of the TG. Toh ref. 4020.

44 _____ . *Shes-rab kyi pha-rol tu phyin-pa'i man-ngag gi bstan-bcos mngon-par rtogs-pa'i rgyan zhes-bya-ba'i tsig-le'ur byas-pa (Mngon rtogs rgyan) (Abhisamayālaṃkāra-nāmaprajñāpāramitopedeśaśāstrakārikā),* ff. 1a-13a, vol 1. (ka) in the Shes-phyin section of the TG. Toh ref. 3786.

45 (SKYABS-RJE PHA-BONG-KHA-PA RJE-BTZUN) BYAMS-PA BSTAN-'DZIN 'PHRIN-LAS RGYA-MTSO (DPAL BZANG-PO). *Bcom-ldan-'das dpal rDo-rje 'jigs-byed dpa'-bo gcig-pa'i sgrub-thabs bdud las rnam-rgyal gyi ngag-'don nag-'gros blo-dman las-dang-po-pa la khyer bde-bar bkod-pa bzhugs-so,* pp. 377-451 in *Bla-ma'i rnal-'byor dang yi-dam khag gi bdag-bskyed sogs zhal-'don gces-btus bzhugs-so.* Dharamsala, India: Tibetan Cultural Printing Press, 1985, 704 pp.

46 _____ . *rDo-rje 'chang Pha-bong-kha-pa dpal bzang-pos lam-gtzo'i zab-khrid stzal-skabs kyi gsung-bshad zin-bris lam-bzang sgo-'byed ces-bya-ba bzhugs-so.* Lhasa printing sponsored by Lha-klu family, c. 1930, 41 ff. Comprises pp. 375-455 in vol. 8 (nya) of collected works, New Delhi: Chophel Legden under the guidance of Kyabje Trijang Rin-poche, 1973.

47 _____ . *rNam-grol lag-bcangs su stod-pa'i man-ngag zab-mo tsang la ma-nor-ba mtsungs-med chos-kyi rgyal-po'i thugs-bcud byang-chub lam gyi rim-pa'i nyams-khrid kyi zin-bris gsung-rab kun gyi bcud-bsdus gdams-ngag bdud-rtzi'i snying-po zhes-bya-ba bzhugs-so (Lam-rim rnam-grol lag-bcangs).* Blocks at dGa'-ldan Monastery, Mundgod, India: Indian recarving sponsored by sKyabs-rje Khri-byang

rin-po-che Blo-bzang ye-shes bstan-'dzin rgya-mtso, c. 1974, 392 ff.

48 *Bye-brag tu rtogs-par byed-pa chen-po (Mahāvyutpatti)*, 2 vols. Tokyo: ed. Ryōzaburō Sakuki, 1962. Also at ff. 1a-131a, vol. 125 (co) in the sNa-tsogs section of the TG. Toh ref. 4346.

49 *('Phags-pa) Blo-gros mi-zad-pas bstan-pa zhes-bya-ba theg-pa chen-po'i mdo (Āryākṣayamatinirdeśanāmamahāyāna-sūtra)*, ff. 122b-270b, vol. 14 (pha) in the mDo-mang section of the KG. Toh ref. 175.

BLO-BZANG GRAGS-PA: see (rGyal-ba rJe) Tzong-kha-pa (chen-po Blo-bzang grags-pa)

50 (PAṆ-CHEN) BLO-BZANG CHOS KYI RGYAL-MTSAN (DPAL BZANG-PO). *Byang-chub lam gyi rim-pa'i dmar-khrid thams-cad mkhyen-par bgrod-pa'i bde-lam zhes-bya-ba bzhugs-so (bDe-lam)*. N.p., n.d., woodblock edition on Tibetan paper in possession of Geshe Lobsang Tharchin, 31 ff. Toh ref. 5944.

51 _____ . *Zab-lam bla-ma mchod-pa'i cho-ga bde-stong dbyer-med-ma (Bla-ma mchod-pa)*, pp. 39-68 of *Bla-ma'i rnal-'byor dang yi-dam khag gi bdag-bskyed sogs zhal-'don gces-btus bzhugs-so*. Dharamsala, India: Tibetan Cultural Printing Press, 1985, 704 pp.

52 (THU'U-BKVAN DHARMA BADZRA) BLO-BZANG CHOS KYI NYI-MA. *Collected Works, Vol. 1 (Ka)*. New Delhi: Ngawang Gelek Demo, 1969, 966 pp. (10 vols. total).

53 (DBEN-SA-PA) BLO-BZANG DON-GRUB. *Rang la gdam-pa bde-chen gter-mdzod sogs thor-bu skor*, ff. 20b-35a, vol. 1 (ka) of collected works. New Delhi: Don-'grub rdo-rje, 1976, 131 pp.

54 (PAṆ-CHEN) BLO-BZANG YE-SHES. *Byang-chub lam gyi rim-pa'i dmar-khrid thams-cad mkhyen-par bgrod-pa'i myur-lam zhes-bya-ba bzhugs-so (Myur-lam)*. Modern Indian reprint sponsored by Blo-bzang dpal-sgron, concluding prayer by sKyabs-rje Gling rin-po-che, 87 ff. Toh ref. 6980.

55 (SKYABS-RJE KHRI-BYANG RIN-PO-CHE) BLO-BZANG YE-SHES

BSTAN-'DZIN RGYA-MTSO, ed. *Rigs dang dkyil-'khor rgya-mtso'i khyab-bdag He-ru-ka: dpal ngur-smrig gar-rol skyabs-gcig Pha-bong-kha-pa bDe-chen snying-po dpal bzang-po'i rnam-par thar-pa don-ldan tsangs-pa'i dbyangs-snyan zhes-bya-ba bzhugs-so*, pp. 5-592 of vol. I, pp. 1-542 of vol. II. New Delhi: Ngawang Sopa, 1981.

DBEN-SA-PA: see (dBen-sa-pa) Blo-bzang don-grub

56 (DPAL) MAR-ME MDZAD YE-SHES (DĪPAMKARA ŚRĪJÑĀNA). *bDen-pa gnyis la 'jug-pa (Satyadvayāvatāra)*, ff. 71b-73a, vol. 30 (a) in the dBu-ma section of the TG. Toh ref. 3902.

57 _____ . *Byang-chub lam gyi sgron-ma (Bodhipatha-pradīpa)*, ff. 242a-245a, vol. 32 (khe) in the dBu-ma section of the TG. Toh ref. 3947 (also found at 4465).

58 (KARMA-PA) MI-BSKYOD RDO-RJE. *mChog-gi dngos-grub mngon-du byed-pa'i myur-lam bka'-brgyud bla-ma rnams kyi rdo-rje'i mgur-dbyangs ye-shes char-'bebs rang-grol lhun-grub bde-chen rab-'bar nges-don rgya-mtso'i snying-po (bKa'-brgyud mgur-mtso)*. Sikkim: Rumtek Monastery, modern reprint, 142 ff.

59 RMOG-LCOG SPRUL-SKU. *Lam gyi gtzo-bo rnam gsum gyi mchan-'grel bzhugs-so*, pp. 2-9 of the collection *Lam gyi gtzo-bo rnam gsum dang de'i 'grel-pa, lta-mgur a-ma ngo-'dzin dang de'i 'grel-pa, rMog-lcog gsung-mgur rnams gzhugs-so*. N.p., n.d.: set in movable type in Western book form, printing prayer by Nang-sog P'a-ru'ang su-nyid-shog gi mchog-sprul Chos-rje bla-ma et al., 35 pp.

60 (RGYAL-BA RJE) TZONG-KHA-PA (CHEN-PO BLO-BZANG GRAGS-PA). *sKyes-bu gsum gyi nyams-su blang-ba'i byang-chub lam gyi rim-pa (Lam-rim chung-ba)*, pp. 4-406, vol. 14 (pha) of collected works. New Delhi: reprint sponsored by Geshe Lobsang Tharchin, 1979. Toh ref. 5393.

61 _____ . *mNyam-med Tzong-kha-pa chen-pos mdzad-pa'i byang-chub lam-rim che-ba (Lam-rim chen-mo)*, pp. 33-1077, vol. 13 (pa) of collected works (ibid). Toh ref. 5392.

62 _____ . *rJe-btzun 'Jam-pa'i dbyangs kyi lam gyi gnad rJe Red-mda'-ba la shog-dril du phul-ba bzhugs-so*, pp. 671-81, vol. 14 (pha) of collected works (ibid). Toh ref. 5397.

63 _____ . *Byang-chub lam gyi rim-pa'i nyams-len gyi rnam-gzhag mdor-bsdus (Lam-rim bsdus don)*, pp. 308-13, vol. 2 (kha) of collected works (ibid). Toh ref. 5275 (59).

64 _____ . *Byang-chub sems-dpa' sems-dpa' chen-po rTag-tu ngu'i rtogs-pa brjod-pa'i snyan-dngags dpag-bsam gyi ljon-pa zhes-bya-ba*, pp. 397-444, vol. 2 (kha) of collected works (ibid). Toh ref. 5275 (70).

65 _____ . *Byin-rlabs nye-brgyud kyi bla-ma rnams la gsol-ba 'debs-pa dngos-grub kyi snye-ma (mKhyen srid ma)*, pp. 206-8, vol. 2 (kha) of collected works (ibid). Toh ref. 5275 (2).

66 _____ . *Bla-ma lnga-bcu-pa'i rnam-bshad slob-ma'i re-ba kun-skong zhes-bya-ba*, pp. 315-71, vol. 1 (ka) of collected works (ibid). Toh ref. 5269.

67 _____ . *Bla-ma dBu-ma-pa la mDo-khams su phul-ba'i chab-shog*, pp. 334-7, vol. 2 (kha) of collected works (ibid). Toh ref. 5275 (65).

68 _____ . *Lam gyi gtzo-bo rnam gsum*, pp. 584-6, vol. 2 (kha) of collected works (ibid). Toh ref. 5275 (85).

69 _____ . *Tsa-kho-ba mKhan-chen Ngag-dbang grags-pas phrin-yig springs byung-ba'i lan*, pp. 580-4, vol. 2 (kha) of collected works (ibid). Toh ref. 5275 (84).

70 (SER-SNGAGS) TSUL-KHRIMS DAR-RGYAS. *dPal 'Khor-lo sdom-pa grub-chen Dril-bu zhabs-lugs lha-lnga'i sgrub-dkyil gyi cho-ga'i chog-bsgrigs bde-chen 'dod-'jo'i bum-bzang zhes-bya-ba las mngon-rtogs kyi rim-pa bzhugs-so.* Lhasa: printing sponsored by sMin-skyid chos-sgron, "1921", 46 ff.

71 (SLOB-DPON) ZHI-BA LHA (ŚĀNTIDEVA). *Byang-chub sems-dpa'i spyod-pa la 'jug-pa (Bodhisattvacaryāvatāra)*, ff. 1a-39a, vol. 26 (la) in the dBu-ma section of the TG. Toh ref. 3871.

72 (DPAL-LDAN) ZLA-BA GRAGS-PA (CANDRAKĪRTI). *Byang-chub sems-dpa'i rnal-'byor spyod-pa bzhi-brgya-pa'i rgya-cher 'grel-pa (Bodhisattvayogācāryacatuḥśatakaṭīkā)*, ff. 29a-236a, vol. 24 (ya) in the dBu-ma section of the TG. Toh ref. 3865.

73 _____ . *dBu-ma rtza-ba'i 'grel-pa tsig-gsal ba zhes-bya-ba*

(Mūlamadhyamakavṛttiprasannapadānāma), ff. 1a-197a, vol. 23 ('a) in the dBu-ma section of the TG. Toh ref. 3860.

74 ———— . *dBu-ma la 'jug-pa zhes-bya-ba (Madhyamakāvatāranāma)*, ff. 198a-216a, vol. 23 ('a) in the dBu-ma section of the TG. Toh ref. 3861.

75 *('Phags-pa) 'Od-srung gi le'u zhes-bya-ba theg-pa chen-po'i mdo (Āryakāśyapaparivartanāmamahāyānasūtra)*, ff. 211a-260b, vol. 6 (cha) in the dKon-brtzegs section of the KG. Toh ref. 87.

76 (RGYAL-BA) YANG-DGON-PA (RGYAL MTSAN DPAL) (LHA GDONG-PA). *Phyag-rgya chen-po lhan-cig skyes-sbyor gyi thon-chos bzhugs-so*, pp. 207-242 in vol. 1 (ka) of collected works. Thimphu, Bhutan: Kunsang Topgey, 1976, 570 pp.

77 (TSE-MCHOG GLING YONGS-'DZIN) YE-SHES RGYAL-MTSAN. *rJe'i thug-sras Tsa-kho dbon-por grags-pa mKhan-chen Ngag-dbang grags-pa'i skor*, pp. 830-2, vol. 1 of *Byang-chub lam gyi rim-pa'i bla-ma brgyud-pa'i rnam-par thar-pa rgyal-bstan mdzes-pa'i rgyan-mchog phul-byung nor-bu'i phreng-pa zhes-bya-ba bzhugs-so*. New Delhi: Ngawang Gelek Demo, 1970, 947 pp.

78 ———— . *Lam gyi gtzo-bo rnam-pa gsum gyi khrid-yig lam-bzang gsal-ba'i sgron-me*, pp. 1-91 in vol. 5 of collected works. New Delhi: Tibet House Library, 1974, 445 pp. Toh ref. 5987.

79 ———— . *Lam gyi gtzo-bo gsum gyi snying-po'i gnad ston-pa'i man-ngag skal-ldan 'jug-ngog*, pp. 345-437 in vol. 19 of collected works (ibid), 488 pp. Toh ref. 6094.

80 (LCANG-SKYA ROL-PA'I RDO-RJE) YE-SHES BSTAN-PA'I SGRON-ME. *Grub-pa'i mtha'i rnam-par bzhag-pa gsal-bar bshad-pa thub-bstan lhun-po'i mdzes-rgyan zhes-bya-ba*. Sarnath, Varanasi, India: The Pleasure [*sic*] of Elegant Sayings Printing Press, 1970, 545 pp.

81 *('Phags-pa) Yongs-su mya-ngan las 'das-pa chen-po'i mdo (Āryamahāparinirvāṇanāmasūtra)*, vols. 1 (ka, 528 ff.) and 2 (kha, 529 ff.) in the Myang-'das section of the KG, etc. Toh ref. 119.

82 (SLOB-DPON) RATN'A-KA-RA SHANTI (RATNĀKARAŚĀNTIPA). *dPal gShin-rje dgra-nag-po'i rgyud kyi rgyal-po chen-po'i dka'-'grel rin-po-che'i sgron-ma (Śrīkṛṣṇayamārimahātantrarājapañjikāratnapradīpanāma)*, ff. 124b-173b, vol. 174 (bi) in the rGyud section of the TG. Toh ref. 1919.

82A (SLOB-DPON) SH'AKYA BLO (ŚĀKYABUDDHI). *Tsad-ma rnam-'grel gyi 'grel-bshad (Pramāṇavārttikaṭīkā)*, vols. 97 (je, 319 ff.) and 98 (nye, 287 ff.) in the Tsad-ma section of the TG. Toh ref. 4220.

83 (*'Phags-pa*) *Shes-rab kyi pha-rol tu phyin-pa brgyad-stong-pa (Āryāṣṭasāhasrikaprajñāpāramitā)*, ff. 1b-450a, vol. 1 (ka) in the brGyad-stong section of the KG. Toh ref. 12.

84 (*'Phags-pa*) *Shes-rab kyi pha-rol tu phyin-pa sdud-pa tsigs-su bcad-pa (Sher-phyin mdo sdud-pa) (Āryaprajñāpāramitāsañcayagathā)*, ff. 189a-215a, vol. 1 (ka) in the Sher-phyin sna-tsogs section of the KG. Toh ref. 13.

85 (SLOB-DPON) SANGS-RGYAS BSKYANGS (BUDDHAPĀLITA). *dBu-ma rtza-ba'i 'grel-pa Buddha-p'a-li-ta (Buddhapālitamūlamadhyamakavṛtti)*, ff. 154b-278a, vol. 17 (tza) in the dBu-ma section of the TG. Toh ref. 3842.

86 (RGYUD-CHEN) SANGS-RGYAS RGYA-MTSO, comp. *dGe-ldan snyan-brgyud kyi man-ngag las byung-ba'i bla-ma'i rnal-'byor dGa'-ldan lha-brgya-mar grags-pa bzhugs-so (dGa'-ldan lha-brgya-ma)*, pp. 11-14 in *Chos-spyod zhal-'don nyer-mkho phyogs-bsdebs bzhugs*. Varanasi, India: W'a-na mtho-slob dge-ldan spyi-las khang, 1979, 352 pp.

87 (*dPal*) *gSang-ba 'dus-pa zhes-bya-ba rgyud-kyi rgyal-po chen-po (Śrīguhyasamājamahātantrarājanāma)*, ff. 431b-536a, vol. 4 (nga) in the rGyud section of the KG. Toh ref. 442.

88 (DGE-SLONG) BSOD-NAMS LHA'I DBANG-PO. *dPe-chos rin-chen spungs-pa'i gsal-byed rin-po-che'i sgron-me'am gtam-brgyud rin-chen phreng-mdzes su grags-pa bzhugs-so*. Dharamsala, India: Tibetan Cultural Printing Press, n.d.; dedication by sKyabs-rje Khri-byang rin-po-che, 278 pp.

89 LHA-GRI SGANG-PA. *bKa'-gdams kyi man-ngag be'u bum sngon-po'i 'grel-pa*. Bir, India: Tsondu Senge, 1976, 481 pp.

(JO-BO RJE DPAL-LDAN) A-TI-SHA: see (dPal) Mar-me-mdzad ye-shes.

B. Works in English

90 CHANDRA, LOKESH. *Buddhist Iconography.* New Delhi: Aditya Prakashan, 1987, 2 vols.

91 DAS, SARAT CHANDRA. *A Tibetan-English Dictionary.* Reprint New Delhi: Motilal Banarsidass, 1970, 1353 pp.

92 EDGERTON, FRANKLIN. *Buddhist Hybrid Sanskrit Grammar and Dictionary, Volume II: Dictionary.* Reprint New Delhi: Motilal Banarsidass, 1972, 627 pp.

93 REYNOLDS, VALRAE, et al. *Catalogue of The Newark Museum Tibetan Collection, Volume III: Sculpture and Painting.* Newark: The Newark Museum, 1986, 208 pp.

94 ROERICH, GEORGE N., tr. *The Blue Annals [of 'Gos lo-tzva-ba gZhon-nu dpal, 1392-1481].* Reprint New Delhi: Motilal Banarsidass, 1979, 1275 pp.

95 THARCHIN, GESHE LOBSANG, and ARTEMUS B. ENGLE, tr. *Nāgārjuna's Letter: Nāgārjuna's "Letter to a Friend" with a Commentary by the Venerable Rendawa, Zhön-nu Lo-drö.* Dharamsala, India: Library of Tibetan Works and Archives, 1979, 163 pp.

96 VOSTRIKOV, A.I. *Tibetan Historical Literature,* tr. H.C. Gupta. Calcutta: Indian Studies, Past & Present, 1970, 275 pp.